The Golden Compass

Your Gold Investment Resource Guide

by Graham Spiers

XAMonline, Inc., Cambridge, MA 02141
© 2013 by Sharon A. Wynne. (Text and illustrations)

Published 2013
Printed in the United States
1 2 3 4 5 6 7 13 12 11 10 09 08

This book is intended to educate and provide general information about personal finances and investments. The author, editor and publisher should not, however, be construed to be engaged in rendering investment, brokerage, legal, tax, accounting, or other professional services by publishing this book. All questions and decisions about your finances and investments should be addressed directly with your qualified financial professional, including your investment broker, accountant and attorney. Accordingly, you are encouraged to consult your personal financial professionals before adopting any of the suggestions in this book or drawing inferences from it. With any investment strategy you select, always remember that past performance does not guarantee or predict future results.

While the author, editor and publisher have endeavored to prepare an accurate and helpful book, they make no representations or warranties, express or implied, with respect to the accuracy or completeness of its contents and specifically disclaim any warranties of merchantability or fitness for a particular purpose. The author, editor and publisher do not assume and hereby disclaim any liability to any party for any loss, damage or injury caused, directly or indirectly, by any error, omission or information provided in this book.

The names, conditions and identifying details of people associated with the events and advice described in this book have been changed to protect their privacy. Any similarities to actual individuals are merely coincidental.

To obtain permission(s) to use the material from this work for any purpose, including workshops or seminars, please submit a written request to:

Lesson Ladder: an imprint of XAMonline, Inc.
25 First Street, Suite 106
Cambridge, MA 02141
Fax: 1-617-583-5552
Email: customerservice@lessonladder.com
Web: www.lessonladder.com

Text: Graham Spiers
Contributing Author: Rick Colella

Illustrations: Images in chapter 10, pages 158 and 159 copyright © J.P. Morgan Asset Management. The use of these charts in no way implies the endorsement, sponsorship, or affiliation of J.P. Morgan Asset Management with this product.

Library of Congress Catalog Card Number: (pending)

Spiers, Graham.
    The golden compass: your gold investment resource guide.

    153 pp., ill.
        1.   Title. 2. Gold. 3. Gold – Purchasing.   4. Investments.
        5. Precious Metals.   6.   Metals as an Investment.

    HG 293 S6547 2012   332.63 Sp445 2012
    ISBN: 978-0-98486-57-2-7

Contents

The Golden Compass

Your Gold Investment Resource Guide

by Graham Spiers

Chapter 1

Gold: The Tears of the Gods

Gold that was picked up by Paleolithic humans twenty thousand years ago is still changing hands today. Gold excavated by slaves in the ancient mines of Nubia has traveled through time and space to reside in the steel vaults of Zurich, Switzerland; the jewelry boxes of India; and the private collections of individual investors around the world. Pulled from rivers; melted down into idols and worshiped; traded for salt, silk, cattle, cocoa beans, and *people;* gold has been circulating as a precious commodity for thousands and thousands of years. Called the "tears of the gods" by the great Incan people of Peru, *gold is on the move once again.*

For the past decade, gold and silver prices have been on a *breathtaking ascent* and have recently reached some of the highest recorded summits in modern history. On September 1st, 2011, the price of gold per troy ounce hit $1,822.80, nearly *nine* times its 2001 average of $207.04. The World Gold Council has determined that gold hit never-before-seen highs *twenty-two times in 2010 alone.* Back in December of 2001, gold's partner, silver, was averaging only $4.50 an ounce; by 2011, silver had jumped well *over nine record times* to $42 an ounce.

Many investors speculate that the values of gold and silver, through the simple law of supply and demand, will rise even further. Certainly, those who invested in these two precious metals ten years ago are feeling euphoric now. Yet, how can these prices sustain themselves? Won't the gold and silver bubbles burst just like technology stocks or the real estate market? Or, are gold and silver *timeless storehouses of value* that have provided protection against economic calamity for thousands of years?

History has shown us that the strength or weakness of the global economy determines the value of these iconic precious metals. Rising gold and silver prices often *coincide* with weakening currencies and economic uncertainty. While the past shows us that gold and silver markets have their natural ups and downs, it also shows that those fluctuations can be *extreme* when governments get involved. Will new industrial uses of both gold and silver stabilize their market presence and create enduring opportunities for 21st century investors? Or, will gold and silver again become the currency of last resort when financial centers collapse and political power games get ugly?

The story of gold and silver is a fascinating one and one that every modern investor should know. In this book, you will find answers to those questions on everyone's mind:

- Why is the price of gold and silver increasing so quickly and dramatically in such a short period of time?
- What do recent increases in gold prices tell us about the future of the country and the world economy?
- Why are so many people turning to gold and silver as a safe haven for their money and as a hedge against economic disaster?
- What should an individual investor know about gold and silver before talking with their investment advisor?

Chapter 2

The Timeless Relevance
of Gold and Silver

Billions of years ago many of the heaviest elements, including gold and silver, were created within the nuclear centers of dying stars called supernovas. Incredible explosions dispersed these elements throughout the galaxies; and on Earth gold and silver were evenly, and widely, distributed. For this reason, cultures on all of the inhabited continents have come into contact with gold and silver, mined them, and used them in similar ways.

As the metals of the gods and the DNA of all currency, gold and silver have, for at least eight thousand years, determined the health and power of the world's civilizations. Empires have scoured the earth with passion for these precious metals, leading to a variety of legendary repercussions. Gold and silver have also transcended their monetary usage by providing industrial, medicinal, and decorative benefits.

Gold

Gold is widely believed to have been the first metal discovered by humans. Most gold appears naturally in an unadulterated state, meaning it is not combined with other minerals like copper or iron. *Placer gold,* or gold that has weathered away from its host rock, was zealously collected as nuggets and dust in the riverbeds and streams of the ancient world.

Gold must have really caught the eye of prehistoric humans: shiny and bright even when dry; luminous yellow, unexpectedly heavy for its size. It never tarnished, never lost its luster. Gold seemed *timeless*. With such excellent malleability it was quite easy to form into shapes. Not surprisingly, the jewelry of many ancient peoples began to include a lot of gold. This delightful material was so completely different from anything else found in nature that gold appeared to be of the gods, and just as sacred.

Gold conveyed *power* and infinite value and soon, within the most important ancient cultures, only those individuals who had power and status were allowed to wear it; it is at this point roughly ten thousand years ago that the perception of gold changed. What was once merely an exciting curiosity collected while combing the local creeks for food, became instead a *symbol* of both spiritual and secular *supremacy*; a symbol that, over the millennia, humans have waged wars over and died for.

Gold as an Object of Worship

Humans have long believed that gold held vital connections to creation, the gods, and an afterlife. In Varna, Bulgaria, a vast Copper Age cemetery 6,500 years old has revealed a culture that was separated into distinctly different social classes. Discovered in 1972, the resting places of many of these prehistoric Bulgarians were relatively plain. The graves of a few inhabitants, however, included *extraordinary* pieces of gold worked into beautiful jewelry, cups, and scepters. One grave held the skeleton of a man of considerable height holding an axe of gold and stone in his hand. Many pieces of pure gold adorned his remains, *clear symbols of power*. It certainly appeared as if this gentleman wanted to take these items with him into the afterlife.

The Varna site is the oldest cemetery yet discovered containing gold buried for spiritual reasons. In fact, there are several chambers where no bodies at all have been found—only vast stores of gold and copper items archaeologists believe were destined for the afterlife of wealthy villagers.

Gold has also been found in the tombs of *Egyptian pharaohs* from the first dynasty over four and a half thousand years ago. It was shaped into statues of the various gods worshipped throughout the Mesopotamian between the Tigris and Euphrates rivers. The Bible, too, speaks extensively of gold, first in the book of Genesis, where the general location of Eden is discussed. Eden sits by one of the rivers coming out of "the land of Havilah, where there is gold: and the gold of that land is good."

The early *Minoans* of the island of Crete, who thrived four thousand years ago in the eastern Mediterranean Sea, were expert metal workers. Examples of their masterful works in gold still exist today as elaborately chained necklaces and spiritual figurines. The Bronze Age *Mycenaeans*, who learned from and later replaced the Minoans as masters of the Mediterranean, were also well-known for their sculpted treasures, including the solid gold death mask of Agamemnon, conqueror of Troy. It is with the discovery of the "Gold of Troy", unearthed in Turkey and dating to the third millennia B.C.E., that we observe unique signs of wealth among ordinary citizens (versus just among the ruling elite). In a merchant sector of Troy, a one pound gravy boat of pure gold was discovered, which would be worth roughly $26,000 in today's dollars!

In today's world, the gold industry is crucial to the incomes and survival of over a *hundred million people worldwide*. Three places, in particular, are the most affected: South Africa, China, and India. South Africa has produced over half of the world's gold since the precious metal was discovered there in 1886. However, South Africa was surpassed by China in 2007 as the world's largest producer of gold. China has also been buying gold for its reserves during the past decade.

India is the largest consumer of gold, purchasing an average of 800 tons each year, roughly a third of the world's demand, mostly in the form of jewelry. The country purchases at least 25% of all gold produced annually—just for body ornamentation. With a strong cultural connection to the metal, individual Indian investors purchased, piecemeal, 540 tons of gold in the first half of 2011 alone.

Properties and Uses of Gold

If we melted down all the gold extracted since antiquity it would fill only two Olympic-sized swimming pools! Three quarters of all the gold that people possess has been found in the last one hundred years. Most of those 168,000 tons of gold are still being passed around humanity today as coins, bullion, and in the most popular form: jewelry. In fact, because gold doesn't rust or tarnish, 60% of all gold has been worked into jewelry at some time in its history.

Carats
In jewelry, gold is usually alloyed with other metals in order to modify its malleability and color. The purity of gold is measured in carats. A 100% solid gold necklace would be 24 carats (written as 24k or, known as 1000 fine). When pieces of gold contain copper, silver, or other metals, the *caratage* is downgraded accordingly to 22k (91.7% gold, or 917 fine), 18k (75%, or 750 fine), 14k (58.5%, or 585 fine), and 10k (41.6%, or 416 fine).

It was the ancient Egyptians, over three thousand years ago, who first learned how to beat gold into what we call *gold leaf*, or the paper-thin gilt used to cover otherwise ordinary objects. Extremely dense, yet the most malleable of all metals, one ounce of gold can be pounded into a sheet of leaf 9 square meters, or almost 97 square feet. That same ounce can be worked into a wire five microns wide that would stretch fifty miles. Gold thread is used in embroidery as a decorative element that adds both beauty and value.

Gold is not only highly conductive and the most ductile (able to form into wire) of all metals but is also immune to corrosion. The first transistor in 1947 used gold contacts and the first laser in 1960 incorporated gold-coated mirrors. The use of gold in modern electrical wiring and contacts has grown ever since. For this reason, many appliances such as cell phones, computers, and TVs contain minuscule amounts of gold to help accurately conduct electrical current.

Gold is highly useful in extraterrestrial applications as well. In 1965, the first astronaut to engage in a space-walk used a gold-coated visor to protect his vision from the sun. These visors are standard issue today. Despite its cost, numerous satellites have been coated with a gold/polyester film to protect them from electromagnetic radiation. Gold can be worked to transparency and charged with electricity so it is used to de-ice aircraft cockpit windows.

Gold is non-toxic and has been used in dentistry since the Etruscans of Italy first wired false teeth into the jaws of some very brave patients in 600 B.C.E. Gold fillings have always been desired for their high quality and durability. Gold is also known to have anti-inflammatory properties. It has been used to treat both rheumatoid arthritis and tuberculosis. Radioactive gold is injected into the body for diagnosis of disease and certain gold isotopes are utilized in the treatment of cancer.

The growing industrial and medical uses of gold are adding to its already strong market value. While most gold is still used for jewelry or vaulted away as a store of wealth, 21st century science is innovating gold into new applications based solely on the metal's unique physical properties. Combine this fact with the *scarcity* of gold and you have a *crucial commodity* that will likely become more vital with time. Many analysts are not surprised by the recent rise of gold to almost $1,900 an ounce. In fact, some experts consider it likely that gold will be $10,000 an ounce by the year 2025. Only time will tell.

Gold Mining

Placer gold was the first gold exploited by early civilizations. The riverbeds presented gold in the forms of nuggets and dust and the ancient Greeks (beginning around 800 B.C.E.) used sheepskins to capture the flakes in the rivers of what is now western Turkey. The skins would then be hung to dry, shaken, and beaten until the gold came loose and flickered down from the wool. It is easy to see how this ancient, practical technique became the root of the timeless Greek story of the Golden Fleece.

Mining gold underground was pioneered by the Egyptians around 1500 B.C.E. Areas of Nubia, or modern northern Sudan, were so richly veined that pharaohs were able to use gold not only in religious worship but also as a *medium of exchange* with the rest of the burgeoning eastern Mediterranean world.

The Roman Empire, beginning in the first century B.C.E., was instrumental in furthering the science of gold-mining. Roman engineers first gathered placer gold by using their knowledge of hydraulics and building aqueducts to control rushing streams. They experimented with water-wheels and gates called sluices to trap the heavier gold from the alluvial sands of flood plains. Using slaves captured from continuous warfare, the Romans mined their conquered lands deep underground, using fire to melt and separate the gold from its surrounding ore.

The eighth century A.D. Kingdom of Ghana was the first major power to dominate the mines in western Africa. Gold was used to trade for another vital commodity needed in their hot and humid environment: salt from the Sahara. The early 1300s Malian Empire of Mansa Musa 1st later controlled the gold and salt trade from the Atlantic all the way into Saudi Arabia, delivering the gold to the Middle East that brought back the silks and spices from the Far East lands of Asia.

Silver

Second only to gold among precious metals, silver's history is just as important if only for its *relationship* to the value of gold. Silver in its natural state is most often found alloyed with other metals such as gold, copper, zinc, and lead. Unlike gold, silver often has to be *refined* before it can be used and it took mankind a bit longer to figure out how to do this successfully and efficiently; this metallurgic knowledge increased dramatically through the Copper and Bronze ages several thousand years ago. Once separated into a usable form, silver doesn't disappoint. A white metal, shiny and easily worked, it has long been used for jewelry and eating utensils, the latter because of its antiseptic qualities.

Properties and Uses of Silver

Silver is extremely ductile, meaning it is an excellent conductor of both electrical and thermal energies. It has the lowest contact resistance of any metal, making it very valuable in electronics. Being a transition metal, it attracts free neutrons and is used by the nuclear power industry to make control rods for reactors.

Silver, when highly polished, is the mirror of choice. It is used in solar reflectors and graces the mirrors of the most important telescopes, including the Hubble Telescope. Silver dissolves in nitric acid and the resulting chemical reaction produces silver nitrate, a highly sensitive product used to create photographs since the 19th century.

Fine silver is 99.9% pure, but this grade is usually too soft to work with and is usually alloyed with other metals such as copper to make commodities like *sterling* silver. Sterling silver contains at least 92.5% of the precious metal. In the United States, a product must contain 90% of the precious metal to even be called silver. Silver has a lustrous white shine and it is quite malleable, making it perfect for jewelry and currency. Because silver is a fraction of the price of gold, almost as malleable, and still widely desired, it is more easily and frequently worked by jewelers. Most jewelry is made from sterling silver.

Silver has been found to have antibacterial properties and so it has always been valued in making silverware eating utensils. Even in the 1800s sailors would place silver coins in barrels of water to keep it drinkable. Silver compounds were used to treat wounds during the First World War in order to fight infection. Today, silver sulfadiazine (SSD) cream is used in the treatment of serious burns. Silver is used in hospital catheters. It is added to garments like socks to reduce odors brought on by bacteria and fungi, and since silver interacts with pure air and water without oxidizing, it is also alloyed with other metals to make amalgams used in dental fillings.

Silver is not as scarce as gold. It is the least expensive *precious metal* and is often found while mining for base metals like copper, lead, or zinc. However, silver's many industrial uses complement its lustrous utility as a *store of value*. Investors in silver should know that when the mining industry is going strong, especially in inflationary times with low interest rates, silver's value will increase as it has in the past several years. Conversely, when there are high interest rates, and money supply growth is being constrained by government, mining production typically slows, demand drops and, historically, silver prices fall.

Silver Mining

Most archeologists agree silver was first mined in the central and western parts of modern-day Turkey, as far back as six thousand years ago. Around 3000 B.C.E., the Chaldean culture in this area began to figure out a process to extract silver from lead ore. Many of their mines were in Asia Minor, near present day Armenia, just north of Turkey.

The Laurium mines, near Athens, Greece, expanded the ancient Mediterranean world's trade in silver for over a thousand years. Archeologists believe that in its heyday, beginning in 600 B.C.E., Laurium produced a million ounces of silver each year for almost three centuries.

Carthage, a long-time Phoenician colony on the coast of present-day Tunisia, began exploiting silver deposits in modern-day Spain and Portugal. The Roman Republic took over those mines after more than a hundred years of war with the Carthaginians and minted the silver into coins that became a standard for trade throughout the ancient world. The Roman Empire's silver currency has been found as far away as western Asia.

The hunt for precious metals turned inwards for the West in the eighth century A.D., three centuries after the Roman Empire fell. The Islamic Moors invaded Spain and as a military force isolated Christian Europe from its African and Asian trading partners. As luck would have it, however, much silver was found right in Central Europe, especially in modern-day Germany, Austria, Hungary, and the Czech Republic, making the Western empires less dependent on the East for silver.

At the close of the 15th century, Europe began to look outward again. The Portuguese and Spanish sailed first around Africa and then west into the Atlantic looking for spices, slaves, gold, and silver. With the conquest of both the Aztec and Inca Empires in the New World in the early 16th century, the Spanish inundated themselves with priceless, captured jewelry and relics. All of it was melted down and molded into bars that sailed back across the Atlantic into the coffers of the Spanish kings.

Gold and Silver Discoveries in the United States

The state of North Carolina was the scene of the first gold rush on United States soil. First, in 1799, a 17 pound gold nugget was found in that state's *Cabarrus County*. A rush began in earnest when gold was found in Little Meadow Creek in 1803. By 1828 the U.S. Mint in Philadelphia was using gold solely from North Carolina.

The *California Gold Rush of 1848-49* created a surge in the amount of the precious metal in North America. By 1852, California gold production was at an annual rate of $81 million. This was at a time when gold was $18.93 a troy ounce! With such tremendous possibilities for wealth came equally momentous consequences for the U.S., Mexico, and the Southwest's indigenous populations. After hundreds of thousands of people from all over the globe moved to the California Territory in just a few years, bloody wars erupted between Native American tribes and prospectors. The region was also experiencing the displacement and marginalization of Native and Hispanic cultures, a result of a short but bloody war between Mexico and the United States in 1846-48. The Mexican Cession, a political consequence of this conflict, affected the entire southwest, bringing California, Texas, and several other states into the Union.

A dramatic discovery of gold and silver in modern day Virginia City, Nevada—what became known as the *Comstock Lode*—occurred in 1859. While millions of dollars in precious metals were discovered, the Comstock Lode is most renowned for the innovations in mining that occurred from getting to and refining the ore. Veterans of Mexican silver mines and highly trained German engineers worked with those who had experienced the California Rush to advance extraction and smelting techniques. The Comstock Lode also financed the Union effort during the American Civil War of 1861-65 with plenty of silver and gold for weapons and supplies, giving the north a strong advantage.

Coming Chapters...

The relationship between humans and precious metals stretches back thousands and thousands of years. We have sought to possess it, have waged wars over it, adorned ourselves with it, and financed our civilizations with it since even before the written record. This enduring relationship exists even today and the modern investor may do well to understand the timeless relevance of gold.

In chapters 3, 4, 5, and 6 we will discuss the various gold and silver investment products available to the modern investor and how and where they can be purchased; we will explore the options for storing your precious metals; and we will review the current regulations concerning ownership and investment in gold and silver.

For those also interested in the long, fascinating history of gold, its complicated relationship with money, its role as the economy's thermometer, and the up and down saga of the gold standard, see chapters 7, 8, and 9.

Chapter 10 provides a review and summary of the generally accepted pros and cons of investing in gold and silver and chapter 11 provides gold and silver "Top Ten" lists.

Chapter 3

Choosing the Right Gold or Silver Product for You

Many experts agree that an investment portfolio should include at least a 10-15% allocation to precious metals; however, the modern investor has many gold and silver products to choose from, so how should they choose? This chapter reviews the pros and cons of the vast array of gold and silver products available and evaluates how they each measure up as tools for portfolio diversification.

Diversifying Your Portfolio

Creating a diversified portfolio is the wisest thing an investor can do. An investor should have a good *mix* of stocks, bonds, gold, and cash, among other investment products such as real estate. With a diversified portfolio, if one asset decreases significantly in value, chances are there will be other assets in the portfolio that will hold up and keep the investor from experiencing steep losses. Thus a thoughtfully diversified portfolio supports *asset preservation*.

There are three basic rules for investing:

1. The potential returns you can expect from your portfolio are directly related to *the amount of risk* that you take. So be sure to think long and hard about your investment goals and pick a risk level you can live with through good times and bad.
2. The degree of risk that you take is directly related to the quality of *your research* on the assets you hold. Determine how each asset can be expected to perform in different market environments.
3. If you properly *diversify* your investment portfolio, you can reduce your risk.

Since this book is about investing in gold and silver, let's say right now that to own a portfolio that was *only* constructed of precious metals and mining stocks would *not* be a good strategy! However, here are some options to discuss with your licensed investment advisor about products you may want to buy relating to gold and silver.

Physical Gold and SIlver

The first product option would be *physical* gold and silver. You can touch physical gold and silver and hold it in your hand. Gold and silver are great diversifying assets and are helpful for achieving asset preservation. In the worst of times, precious metals have historically performed well when most other assess have lost value. Physical precious metals are also easier to *liquidate* or sell. And that's the irony: even though gold and silver are forever, you want to be able to sell them quickly if need be and turn them into the currency of your choice at the best possible price.

Physical gold and silver come in two types for investors: coins and bars. There are many varieties of each and it pays to do some research to find out which is best for you. If you wish to invest in a lot of gold and silver, for both the long and short term, it would be best to buy both coins (in modern denominations and in pre-1933 collector coins) and bullion bars that range in *various sizes* so they can be liquidated more easily.

> Note:
> Please keep in mind that the prices indicated here can change day to day and may not reflect the price of the product on the day you are reading this book.

Bullion Coins

Most experts believe the best investments in gold and silver are coins. Coins are easily purchased and are easily authenticated. They are portable, efficiently stored and, because they are negotiable currency, are more easily redeemed than bars. Coins can be kept at home, safely, and available for emergencies. In short, if you can get to them easily enough, they are the best insurance against catastrophic events.

One ounce bullion coins are the most popular coins. They are sold by governments around the world to raise cash; they are actually a source of *national pride* as their fine details bear the craftsmanship of local artists and engravers. Governments make them available from time to time directly from their mints; but, an investor usually purchases them from a retail firm specializing in gold coins.

The disadvantage in buying coins from a retail firm is the price markup *above* the daily London Fix price. Sometimes the markup can be between eight and ten percent! For example, if your coin is made of an ounce of fine gold, at $1,800 an ounce, the retailer will add the following to the price:

- seigniorage, a term used to describe the costs the original mint charges for production of the coin (up to 3%)
- a wholesale markup (a small percentage)
- a dealer's retail markup of up to 5%
- and any state tax that might apply

So, let's see how this extra mark-up on gold's daily price plays out: A 1986 U.S. Mint, one ounce, American Eagle Proof Gold $50 coin could be had for just a little under *$2,500* in September 2011. That's almost $700 over gold's actual price per ounce! Yes, it is a proof coin, something we'll go over very soon. True, the coin is both a collectible *and* an ounce of gold but what if gold tumbles in the market next week? Well, the coin will always be worth at least the fifty dollar face value; and it would be highly unlikely that gold would go down below $100 an ounce anytime soon (it hasn't since 1973, before gold became legal for Americans to purchase). Plus, it is a collector's item and that counts towards its value. Luckily, if you'd like something a bit less risky, you can also purchase non-proof gold coins in one ounce, 1/2, 1/4, and 1/10 ounce denominations.

One thing to remember about coins is that none are *pure* gold because pure gold is just too soft for currency. Coins have rates of *fineness,* or the pure gold weight ratio per 1000 parts. Many, like the American Eagle or the South African Krugerrand, can be 91.6% gold (rated 916 fine, or 22 carat) or 90% (900 fine, or 20 carat). However, the most popular coins on the market today, the Austrian Philharmonic, the Canadian Maple Leaf, the American Golden Buffalo, the Australian Kangaroo, and the recently released Chinese Panda, are .999% gold, or 24 carat.

Silver dollar coins had always been used as regular dollars by the U.S. citizen until recently when the U.S. Mint made regular dollars much smaller, lighter, and of a much cheaper alloy for 21st century use. So real silver dollars have become investments again, as they were in the old days when they were given as gifts for the birth of a child or on subsequent birthdays. Presently, with silver just under $40 an ounce, plus the mark-ups we've discussed, an investor can purchase a 2008 U.S. Mint American Silver Eagle one ounce silver coin for just under $50. Silver coins, like gold coins, can also be had at lower weights and denominations of silver.

Collectibles

Another idea to remember about purchasing coins is that *collectible* coins, or coins that have a face value apart from their metallic make-up, are evaluated and sold a bit differently than bullion coins. Collectible coins have a value that is added based on their *scarcity*, or how rare they are, and the *grade*, or condition of the coin. A grade of 64 to 70 on a coin means that they are in great shape, with 70 being the highest (the coin looks like it was just minted) and, by far, the rarest.

Collectible coins are evaluated by their *mint state* (MS) or their condition once removed from the U.S. Mint. All coins have bag marks, or little nicks and cuts caused by other coins while being carried around in a bag for delivery. All coins, if handled in commerce, wear and smooth at least a little bit; that's the nature of metal. So, a grade of MS60 or less would mean a coin displays the effects of being a coin in the marketplace.

A number of coins from each mint year are removed from circulation directly from the Mint for collectible purposes. Some uncirculated coins never enter the marketplace at all because they are simply kept by their first owners specifically for saving. Coins that grade an MS60, or better, present themselves to the collector's eye as an *uncirculated* coin.

> Most brokers would recommend that you invest in coins that are at least MS64 or better.

One last thing about collectible coins: when President Roosevelt signed the 1933 Executive Order 6102, confiscating all gold from American citizens, he allowed two important exceptions. The first exception was jewelry. Americans could own gold jewelry and not be fined or put in jail. The second exception was for pre-1933 coins. If the coin was minted in gold before 1933, the coin was considered a collectible and, therefore, untouchable by Revenue agents. Some experts believe that if the U.S. government ever decided to confiscate gold again, the legal precedent from the 1933 Executive Order would keep these coins safe in the hands of their investors. Is this a sure thing? Of course not; if the government wants your gold, it will get your gold—but it might be that the government would allow collectibles while confiscating most of the other free gold in the country.

Proofs

Proof coins are a different animal altogether and are somewhat artistic pieces so they have value as collectibles in addition to their bullion value. This makes them a riskier investment because they are more difficult to liquidate for as much as they were purchased. Proofs are often pricey to begin with, like the 2008 American Eagle we spoke of earlier. That's because proof coins are *showpieces* for a particular coin design; they're quite beautiful. The dies (the top and bottom metal plates that contain the design) used to stamp the coin are more refined, and the proof coin is often stamped two to three times in order to create a more distinct detail. An acid is used to polish the coin so that its flat surfaces shine like a mirror and its raised surfaces take on a frosted look.

Review: Bullion Coins
• Gold and silver coins are popular investments because they are portable, relatively safe to hold onto at home, and more easily redeemable.
• Coins sometimes hold a value quite apart from their metallic content. If they are collectible items, both rarity and the grade will enter in to the final evaluation of any particular coin.
• Bullion coins can be expensive depending upon the price of gold and silver, additional price mark-ups, and the fineness of the coin.

Bullion Bars

Bars, while beautiful and satisfying to view and hold, can be extremely heavy and difficult to store—and talk about putting all of your eggs in one basket: a typical 400 ounce gold bar would, in late 2011, command $752,000! It would be difficult to feel safe with a commodity like that in your house!

Because of this, bars are usually kept in banks, often in *offshore* banks (meaning outside of U.S. borders) to avoid excessive taxation. Bars are kept as family heirlooms, hedges against the collapse of a homeland's economic system, and are useful when an investor needs to change geographic locales. Bars kept in secure banking institutions or brokerage houses will often be traded for an investor's desired currency. The bars themselves might be delivered to another secure holding place closer to the investor, if the need arises.

Bars come in a variety of forms. Some only weigh a half ounce. The largest are 400 ounces. The smallest types of bars actually look like little, thin candy bars. They are made of sheets of gold and are struck by a press to imprint the weight, purity (fineness), and the name of the producer on the bar. The big gold bars, like those that you see in the movies, are made from molten gold poured into casts that conform to the desired weight. Then, these bars are precision filed to make sure they are exact. Finally, they are stamped with weight, fineness, and the name of the producer, plus a *serial number* to identify them within a vault. Investors with *allocated* gold accounts know their bars because of these serial numbers.

Bars have less overhead incorporated into their price because one is literally buying in bulk depending upon the order; however, with so much money involved, *verification* of a gold bar's *authenticity* is a major issue. This is why gold bars are difficult to liquidate. Many brokers or banks will not purchase a larger bar unless it is already in their possession and has been authenticated with an assay to determine its purity. This takes time. Plus, the buyer will usually only set the price once he has taken delivery and has made the assay. Gold prices change hourly as well as daily, so this could be a huge factor during price fluctuations like in July and August of 2011. Gold and silver bullion bars can be purchased at reputable brokerages, commodities exchanges, and certain banks.

Review: Bullion Bars
• Gold and silver bars consolidate an investor's savings into an internationally recognized hard asset that can be used to transfer extremely large amounts of wealth.
• Bars are expensive because of the amount of pure metal they contain.
• Gold bars are difficult to move and liquidate because of the verification process and the large amount of cash needed for redemption on a large bar.
• They must be stored in a secure venue like a bank or brokerage house of stellar reputation.

Jewelry and Precious Objects

Over 60% of the world's gold has been worked into jewelry at some time. Citizens of India, for instance, will collectively buy many tons of gold each year in order to meet the demand for the wedding season, when the families of brides purchase gold to use in both the ceremony and as a dowry. Jewelry is certainly the most *auspicious* and, perhaps, the most *beautiful* of all gold and silver's uses. Because gold and silver are so malleable, other metals are usually mixed in with them to create a more efficient hardness for artistic endeavors. Therefore, with jewelry, the metallic aspect of its make-up is sometimes devalued because the gold and silver used can range from pure fineness to a minority composite (less than half of the alloy).

Jewelry is usually more valuable in its *artistic* form than when melted down and purified into gold or silver. Usually, the value of a piece will derive from the combination of the fineness of the metals as well as the expertise of the *craftsmanship*. Remember that the fineness of the metals is slightly more crucial in jewelry as an investment though, especially if these pieces need to be turned into cash. The craftsmanship is rarely ever rewarded while haggling with a pawnshop or investment broker unless the piece is exceedingly unique. Chances are that these pieces will be disassembled and melted down to create a more useful value unless the broker is certain the art *as a whole* is more enticing than the possession of the metal.

For antique and precious objects, value is evaluated on a piece by piece basis. Sterling silverware is more valuable as a complete set; although, one can find separated pieces that are much desired as antiques. Silver candlesticks, however, might be melted down for industrial use. Almost any antique object made of 20 to 24 carat gold will keep its value and may even be evaluated as priceless. However, these objects are difficult to assay and authenticate. In present day, 24 carat pure gold is just too expensive and soft for use in artistic endeavors except when pounded into more economical gold leaf and the value of leaf depends upon how the gold is applied, the age of the object, and what the object is used for. Gold leaf's use in religious objects often adds collectable or sentimental value that creates a higher market price than the metal itself.

Review: Jewelry and Precious Objects

- For investment purposes, jewelry has both a metallic value and an artistic value.
- The artistic value is often disregarded when redeeming jewelry unless the piece is quite unique.
- Precious objects are often worth more as antiques, and as complete sets, than as metals.
- Beautiful objects of pure gold or 24 carats are often priceless, especially if they are antiques or of religious value, and are often difficult to assess.

Gold Statement Accounts (Allocated & Unallocated)

You'll learn more about statement accounts later when we discuss storage options for your gold in chapter 5. Suffice to say, at this point, that you can purchase gold and then store it in two common ways at banks and brokerage houses. *Allocated* accounts keep your gold separated from other gold; your serial numbered bars and your coins will be kept in a safety deposit box.

Unallocated accounts give you a specified purchased share of the amount of gold that the bank or brokerage owns. You do not own specific bars, just a percentage.

Gold Certificates

Gold certificates are simply notes that look official, like paper money, and promise redemption of the amount of money, in gold, listed on the certificate when the owner chooses to redeem that note. In the United States, gold certificates were issued between the mid-19th century and 1933 by a ridiculously high number of banks both charted and uncharted, in order for banks and the federal government to raise money against their supplies of gold. As history displays, an uncomfortably high percentage of these institutions failed and certificate owners were left holding worthless paper.

Once private gold ownership was outlawed in the U.S. following the 1934 Gold Reserve Act, gold certificates were simply not allowed to be held by citizens. For this reason most of them were redeemed, and today they are rare, and collectible, if intrinsically worthless.

Some countries, like Germany and Switzerland, have banks that still issue certificates for unallocated gold accounts. This makes gold certificates popular today because investors still want to own gold in their investment portfolios; and, with unallocated account certificates, they don't have to worry about the storage costs. These investors feel that their certificates make their gold highly liquid and that this allows for quick *conversion* into cash when the need arises. Proponents say certificates are safe to keep at home and they also allow for one to receive the benefits of gold ownership without worrying about paying the *premiums,* or markups, for gold coins or bars.

Critics contend that because of *fractional reserve banking,* where a bank only has to store a small percentage of its deposits within its vault, if economic trouble creates a queue of people lining up to redeem their certificates, there will not be enough gold on hand and the investors will be out of luck. Again, this certainly would be a similar disadvantage of both the gold certificate and the unallocated gold deposit account. Detractors also say that certificates can be counterfeited as well as over-issued by disreputable institutions. Also, if even a reputable institution folds, the certificate, being tied to unallocated gold, is worthless.

One particular investment in gold certificates might be noted, however. This is the certificate that is being issued presently by the Western Australian government of Perth. The *Perth Mint* will sell you a minimum certificate of $5000 Australian dollars with minor charges compared to the markups of physical gold. The gold never leaves the Mint's vaults and the Mint does not charge for storage. Your investment is backed by the Perth government and, additionally, Lloyds of London. There is no taxation of any type for buying, holding, or selling of precious metal in Australia. Plus, if you would like to visit Australia and see your gold, even though it is unallocated, give ten days' notice and you can hold what amounts to your investment in your hand.

Review: Gold Certificates

- They allow for liquidity and, because it is unallocated gold, there are no storage costs.
- There are some very good international programs, like the Perth Mint Certificate Program; unfortunately, the vault is in Australia.
- They are only as good as the issuing institution; the institution, even if reputable, only has a fraction of its reserves on hand and, in times of economic stress, may not be able to redeem each issued certificate.
- If the proper research is not done on the institution issuing the certificate, the certificate could become worthless if the institution fails.

Stocks and Mining Companies

Buying stock in a mining company involves a relatively high amount of risk. Mines take time to locate, time to develop and, by their very nature they are exploiting the natural resources of a region. Some people who don't like this exploitation protest, and even sabotage, mining endeavors. Another consideration is that in some nations, government authorities may decide to shut down a mine and keep the reserves for itself in a process called *nationalizing*.

Nonetheless, mining stocks can be quite profitable. You really just need to do your *research*. Is the company a firm with a successful history of finding gold and silver? Is the company a development firm that concerns itself with the actual extraction of the ore or just the exploration end? Go to the company's website and make sure that the firm has a solid list of success and a record of being involved with reliable, ore producing mines. Research the staff, making sure that the administrators of various mining projects have a long list of *achievement* in their fields. The companies should also have a bottom line in the black; they should be making a profit from the mines that they are developing.

Probably the most important aspect within a mining company's prospectus is the amount of *proven reserves* that they believe to be held within their working mines. These reserves should be in the high millions of ounces. At least, then, you would be comfortable giving them your money when the prices of gold and silver are as high as they are today. The mining company would certainly sell their product at a great profit and you would receive a profit, or dividend from their efforts.

Four Types of Mining Companies

There are four types of companies you can invest in. The first group is comprised of the *majors*. They are the largest mining companies that actually extract the precious metals and, to get that big, they must have enjoyed some success. These companies are also listed on the major stock exchanges, so if you know the ticker symbol of the company you are looking for, you can monitor how the stock is doing day to day.

The second group is made up of *development* companies who could be producers or simply preparing the mine for a major company. This is a middle-tier category so when you invest in one of these companies, you simply want growth—meaning that you wish to see the company grow and you gradually buy more stock in the company as a long-term investment.

Exploratory companies are especially risky investments, but research certainly comes in handy here. If you can find a company with talented geologists and managers with a solid record of success, you might have something. These companies should also come with a recommendation from a licensed stock broker.

Finally, *ancillary* companies include companies that own a variety of mines including both precious and base metal mines. These companies are often *conglomerates,* with different businesses operating in various areas of the mining sector. Base metals are often extracted with precious metals as parts of the same ore (especially in silver mining) so it is desirable to own stock in a company that knows how to make the most of its mine.

It is also wise to consider non-U.S. based companies because they might be involved in areas of the globe that have yet be advantageously exploited.

Review: Mining Stocks

- Because of the capital-intensive nature of mining, you need to be careful to pick a company that (1), knows what it's doing; and (2), has proven reserves to draw from.
- There are four types of stocks you can research: the majors, the developmental, the exploratory, and the ancillary mining companies. Decide what your goals are in investing in mining stocks and choose wisely, with the help of a licensed professional.
- Research the country, or countries, where the company has its mines. Does the government have a long history of

cooperation with this company, or mining in general? Is the government stable? What are the possible environmental effects of the mine and, if the mine is in a delicate area, could these effects be potentially catastrophic for the stock?

Commodities Trading, Gold Futures, and Options

Commodities are physical items that are traded in the world's exchanges. Commodities are the basics like oil, pork, and wheat; the things that create gasoline, bacon, and breakfast cereal—the necessities. There are *exchanges* all around the world where merchants try to get the best price for what they're buying and selling. One of the largest commodities exchanges in the world exists in New York City; it is called COMEX, which stands for the New York Commodity Exchange.

The COMEX is an exchange where one can trade gold and silver in a variety of forms. But first, we need to know that gold and silver are actually the *underlying assets*, or the physical commodities that are being traded via derivative investment instruments. When an investor purchases a precious metal derivative instrument, he or she does not usually expect to actually take delivery of that product. Instead, the investor receives a piece of paper (a derivative contract) that explains what has been purchased. These exchange contracts, a form of investment *security*, come in a variety of forms and the two most common forms are called *futures* and *options*.

Futures and options derive their value from the physical commodity, or the underlying asset. This is the reason why futures and options are called *derivatives*. Let's talk about gold futures first (with the knowledge that silver futures are similar).

Gold Futures

Contracts are promises. When you purchase a gold futures contract you are theoretically agreeing to take delivery of a particular quantity of gold from a vendor on a particular date at a predetermined price. If you buy an ounce of gold today for $1800 using a futures contract and the price goes up to $2,300 an ounce by the time you are scheduled to take delivery, you will have earned $500 on that ounce of gold.

Or, since you never expected to actually take delivery, you could make money on that ounce of gold by selling your gold futures contract to someone else before the delivery date. You would then be betting on the price of gold going up and that makes you a *speculator*. Speculating on any commodity can be risky. What if gold tumbles in price as it did between 1980 ($615 average) and 1981 ($460)?

As well, when you purchase a *real* gold futures contract, you agree to purchase not just one ounce, but at least *one hundred ounces*. This is a commodities exchange after all and most participants are either locking in the price (hedging) of large amounts that they have produced and expect to sell in the future, or need large amounts for production in the future and want to lock in their costs today (also called hedging). There are also many thousands of traders who are in the futures market speculating about the future direction of prices. There are literally thousands of trades happening each hour at COMEX, so obviously a more realistic contract quantity would be one hundred ounces, not one ounce. Now, if you own one contract for $1800 and gold goes up to $2,300 an ounce, you have made fifty grand! Or, if the price declines, you might be in serious trouble.

Each exchange, like the COMEX, has its own parameters for its contracts. Each commodity in the exchange has its own standardized type of contract that requires a specific quantity, time span, and price setting to be met between buyer and seller before that contract is validated as legally binding. During the time before a futures contract expires, it is called an *open position*. You are free to sell your open position to someone else at any time before the contract expires. If you don't, you need to pay up and take delivery. Contracts can run from one month to several months depending upon the commodity.

Margins

When you enter into a futures contract, you have to put down a deposit that has been fixed by the exchange. This is called an *initial margin deposit*. It's a percentage of the total delivery price of the contract, usually 2% to 10% of the contract's face value, and can be seen as a legally required act of good faith. In effect the investor is entering into a leveraged investment; a $10 initial margin at a 10% margin level creates an investment exposure worth $100, a leverage of 10 to 1.

The exchange also requires the payment of *maintenance margins*, a daily margin payment that can either flow from the exchange to the investor if the investment goes up in value or, from the investor to the exchange, if the investment goes down in value. Thus, while the investor can control a large investment with a small initial payment (financial leverage), he must pay any loss or will receive any gain in cash on a daily basis. In this way, all contracts are "marked to market" on a daily basis, insuring that all participants can truly "afford" their open positions at the end of every day. If an investor fails to meet a margin call, the exchange will immediately liquidate that investor's open position.

Review: Futures Contracts

- Futures contracts are leveraged investments and are an opportunity that, if worked correctly with plenty of research, can yield short-term high rewards. But leverage can be dangerous if markets move against your position quickly.
- Futures contracts are legally binding contracts for future delivery of an asset and are not actual physical assets. They require deposits of cash that may easily be lost if prices on the commodities tumble below the contract price and the contracts must be sold quickly at a lower price.
- The best thing to do with futures investments is to make sure that you do the research by going to the commodities exchange website of your choice. Then, speak to a licensed broker about the best possibilities in the futures arena.

Options

Options are another way to purchase gold and silver futures with less risk. An option is another type of contract between a buyer and a seller and, like futures, is usually facilitated through an exchange. When buying a call option an investor will pay a *premium*, or a fee, in order to have the right, but not the obligation, to purchase an asset from a seller at an agreed upon price at a set future date. This price is called the *strike price*.

The options contract is only for a *limited time*. If the contract expires and the current market price is below the strike price, the buyer obviously wouldn't exercise his right to buy using his options contract, since the option strike price would be more expensive. So the buyer would let the options contract expire and the premium would be lost. However, if the current market price exceeds the strike price at the expiration of the contract, then the buyer would exercise his right to purchase the asset at the bargain contract price. During the life of the option, if the market price moves above the strike price, the option is said to be *in-the-money* and the investor may choose to sell the option contract for a profit.

Options are *versatile* and an investor can be either buyer or seller, and with practice and experience, both. Note though, that a brokerage account must be opened first to start the process.

Call Options and Put Options

There are two types of options: call options and put options. A *call* option gives the buyer the right, but not the obligation, to buy an asset at a set price for a set time period. A *put* option gives the buyer the right, but not the obligation, to sell an asset at a set price for a set time period. There are many financial strategies utilizing options but it is wise to remember that selling (writing) options is a far more dangerous strategy than buying options. Always consult a financial advisor before entering into any option strategy but be particularly careful about option writing strategies. We will comment only on option purchasing strategies.

As an *example* (all numbers are made up for illustration purposes), assume an investor buys a 90-day call option to purchase gold at $1,500 per ounce (the strike price) when the current market price is $1,450 and pays a premium of 2.5%, or $37.50 per ounce. Now assume that 45 days later the market price has risen to $1,600 (a 10.3% rise in price) and the buyer decides to sell his option. He collects a premium of 10%, or $150 per ounce, and his profit is $112.50 per ounce.

You may ask, why did he only make 7.5% (10% less 2.5%) if the price of gold went up a full 10%? The reason is that *numerous* factors can affect the price of an option and the price change in the underlying commodity, while usually the most important, is not the only factor. There is also market volatility, interest rates, and the time remaining in the original option contract to consider. These factors can often be very confusing so be sure to research options *before* buying and work with an experienced options broker.

> The purchase of put options is virtually identical except the investor is betting that the price will *decline* in the future and is buying the right, but not the obligation, to sell an asset at a set price in the future.

Options are not hard assets, or objects with long-term value. Like futures contracts, the purchase of an option contract involves the initial investment of a premium, a little like an initial margin deposit. But, unlike futures contracts, premiums are a *one-time* payment and there is no obligation to make maintenance margin payments during the life of the contract. For this reason, purchased options are less risky than futures contracts. Options in gold and silver certainly have an exciting place in the wildly fluctuating precious metals market we see today. Nonetheless, always seek the guidance of a licensed professional broker before putting money into futures or options.

Review: Options
• Highly versatile, they have the potential to benefit a buyer or a seller (not both). Remember, selling (writing) options is far more risky than buying options.
• If you own gold and silver stocks, buying a put option can be an effective hedge, or safety net, against quickly declining gold and silver prices.
• If gold and silver prices keep rising, a buyer of call options on these commodities could make money quickly by investing a modest premium at the right strike price.
• Options and futures have different and, sometimes, complicated uses and should be thoroughly researched. Visit a licensed investment broker to investigate these products very carefully.

Gold and Silver Mutual Funds

Mutual funds are usually less risky than single-asset investment products. This is because mutual funds, as the name suggests, are *pooled funds* owned *mutually* by numerous shareholders. Because the funds pool the investments of many smaller investors, they are large enough to own a well diversified group of assets, such as stocks or bonds. Some mutual funds will own numerous types of assets, including commodities and currencies. Some may hold short positions and may also use a limited amount of leverage. The large asset base of mutual funds and the revenues generated from fees allow funds to employ professional managers and analysts to guide the fund—something most individual investors cannot afford by themselves. There are thousands of mutual funds to choose from and hundreds that deal in commodities and precious metals.

Most mutual funds are designed to satisfy a *specific demand*. For example, there are large-cap U.S. stock funds, small-cap international funds, balanced funds that may hold both stocks and bonds, and so on. Mutual funds are a single investment that can be a well diversified portfolio themselves. Within a typical large-cap U.S. stock fund there will be anywhere from 20 to as many as 200 stocks and the objective will typically be to perform as well or better than an index, such as the S&P 500 index or the Russell 1000 index. There are aggressive mutual funds that accept more risk, conservative ones without much risk at all, and everything in between.

Distributions

Mutual funds are required to pay what are called *distributions* once or twice a year. There are many moving parts within a mutual fund (buying and selling of shares throughout the year) that aggregate to the total net profits earned in a given year. Those profits (or losses) are divided by the number of shares in the fund and distributions are then paid out proportionately. Once it is determined what an investor's share is on the *record date*, the checks are sent out on the *payable date*. Investors can take receipt of profits or are given the option of reinvesting their earnings back into the fund by buying more shares. When an investor receives a distribution check, or reinvests their earnings, they must pay the IRS on their individual gain.

Fees

Mutual funds also have two primary fees attached. The first fee type, called a *load*, is actually a brokerage commission the fund pays the selling broker. An investor in a mutual fund will, depending on the fund, either pay a *front end load* (a fee added on to the initial purchase price of the shares) or a *back end load* (a fee deducted when the investor wants to cash out of the fund altogether). If you use a broker to invest in a fund, the broker is paid for their services via these loads. Many times this is reasonable since a broker may be providing significant assistance to the investor. However, sophisticated investors can make the trades themselves and choose to invest directly in *no-load* funds, which carry no fees for brokerage and can save investors money.

The second fee covers *ongoing expenses* and *manager costs*, and is charged to the fund monthly such that all shares experience equal costs. There are obvious business costs to running a mutual fund and successful, proven fund managers can command generous compensation (particularly if they have a strong track record). These ongoing expenses are displayed very prominently when investors are given information about the fund, yet it is important to be aware that all expenses can cut into the net returns of the fund.

Mutual funds are not designed to be short-term buy and sell profit products. In fact, many funds will charge investors 2% to 3% of their investment if they sell before 90 days have elapsed. They are designed to be *long-term investments* and most investors stay invested in them and weather the market cycles of ups and downs. Long-term investors may invest in numerous mutual funds as they build a truly diversified global portfolio managed by professional portfolio managers on their behalf. Mutual funds of mining stocks can be interesting products for precious metals investors because the investor can benefit from both well run companies making profits from their business as well as from rising commodity prices. Always review your research with an investment professional in order to make the best choice for your goals.

Review: Mutual Funds
• They are lower risk vehicles and can be expected to provide more modest returns meant for long-term growth within the context of an investor's personal interest, values, risk-tolerance, and goals.
• They pool the money of many investors and hold numerous assets to help disperse the risk and diversify the investment.
• Investors are responsible for both paying taxes on any gains made by the fund and for fees related to the fund; these fees can cut into overall profitability.

Exchange Traded Funds (ETFs)

ETFs, or exchange-traded funds, are a *hybrid* of mutual funds and stocks. They trade like stocks but they are designed to replicate the performance of a *fixed selection* of securities, like a portfolio of bonds or stocks, which a single investor could not easily buy and maintain himself. In other words, unlike mutual funds, there are no fund managers *actively* adjusting, buying, and selling different stocks or bonds in an attempt to outperform some benchmark index. Rather, ETFs are shares issued by companies, such as Barclay's Bank, for an actual portfolio of fixed securities that they create and manage to provide the promised return. ETF management fees, which are imbedded in the final net performance of the ETF, are far less expensive than mutual fund fees.

When you purchase an ETF, you tie yourself to a group of underlying securities that together comprise a single ETF return, and you're in the instrument on your own. You can buy and sell shares of an ETF like you would any individual stock and there are no early redemption fees as with mutual funds. You can only buy or sell mutual funds at the closing price on a given day. You can buy and sell ETFs all day long as with any common stock. This, of course, gives you more freedom than a mutual fund.

Taxes are lower on ETFs because, unlike mutual funds, securities within the fund are not sold by managers actively to profit the fund, but are simply held to replicate the performance of a target index, so there is far less turnover meaning fewer transactions, less short-term capital gains, and usually lower taxes. Still, you might hope there are gains from the ETF as a whole and these gains are taxed when shares in the ETF are sold by you, just like stock.

Within the world of ETFs there are two types of *gold ETFs*; one designed to track the *price of gold* and one designed to replicate the performance of a portfolio of *gold mining stocks,* sometimes known as a Gold Stocks ETF. We will comment on the ETF that tracks the price of gold. While not a recommendation, we favor the SPDR Gold Trust ETF, ticker symbol GLD. GLD has the highest average daily trading volume and is thus much more liquid. The GLD ETF is produced by State Street Global Advisors (SSGA), a subsidiary of Boston-based State Street Bank. Each GLD share is priced at 10% of the value of gold and is actually backed by gold bullion held by the SPDR Gold Trust in the London vaults of HSBC Bank, USA.

Exchange-traded funds can replicate the performance of entire sections of the market, like the entire S&P 500 stock index, or they can focus on specific sectors, industries, or commodities. There could be many securities all bundled together in a single ETF that deal with precious metals, or the dairy industry, or automobiles, for example. However, you have to do the research and decide which ETF is in the industry or field you expect to grow and profit most. ETFs are also a vehicle allowing the purchase of a share of physical gold but traded like any stock in the stock market. The drawback is, you will never see that gold or hold it yourself, and there have been scandals in regards to ETFs not actually having the amount of gold they claim to hold, so be careful and seek professional advice.

Review: Exchange Traded Funds

- Unlike mutual funds, they are more liquid and easily traded like stocks, but without as many fees or loads. That gives you control and freedom.
- They are bundled like mutual funds, so they can replicate the performance of portfolios of securities like stocks and bonds; however, these securities never change within the ETF like they would if a portfolio manager was managing a mutual fund.
- Like mutual funds, they can be lower risk, and, depending on the particular ETF's relationship to the economy, usually provide modest returns.
- The taxes on ETFs, during the time that you own shares, are normally going to be lower than mutual funds.

Chapter 4

Choosing a Place to Do Business

Now that you have decided you have money to invest in gold, you will want to decide your *reasons* for investing in gold. This is important because your reasoning will determine *where* you will invest in gold and *how much* money you will invest.

You may feel that gold is a good long-term investment because of its intrinsic value, or the value it has had for thousands of years to all people. You may not care if the price of gold declines in the short term—you know that if you buy gold and things go badly economically, your gold will still be there to get you through. With this long-term outlook, physical gold, gold stocks, ETFs, and mutual funds may best be suited for you.

Alternatively, you may feel you want to try your hand at gold and silver speculating in options and futures; you either want to bet that the price of gold will rise even more, or you may want to bet that the price will fall. Now you will need experienced professional advice that is top-notch to navigate the correct path. If you are serious about this investment you will benefit from the advice of a *full-service broker* from a reputable brokerage firm or from an *investment advisor* from a registered investment advisory (RIA) firm.

With your goals and objectives determined, just where do you go to establish a relationship to assist you in your gold and silver investments? There are quite a few options. This chapter focuses on a variety of scenarios and the pros and cons of each.

Private Dealers

Private dealers comprise a wide variety of entrepreneurs from well-established precious metals experts to the collectibles shop in the strip mall, to the corner pawn shop. There are people who do their business solely online and they may be reputable, or not. There are those that have been successful for so long, cutting a niche for themselves over decades based on outstanding customer service, that they have seen no need to expand their customer base electronically. Yet, these days, most dealers have websites for their physical businesses, even Facebook pages! It is easy to do research on them just by sitting in front of your computer.

You certainly want a business that has been around for a long time and has a *competent reputation* for buying and selling precious metals. The best firms have been doing business for ten years or more and didn't just get on the bandwagon when gold hit a thousand dollars per ounce. They will be able to give you the best advice since chances are, they have at least seen the market cycle highs and lows. Even better is the proprietor who specializes only in gold and silver, not just someone who dabbles in the field and sells a plethora of other products.

Doing a *background check* is doing your homework. When you have looked at many businesses and have chosen about five convenient ones that seem to suit your needs, search for them on the *Better Business Bureau* (BBB) website to see if they have any registered complaints. The BBB website will tell you if the business is accredited by the BBB (businesses are under no obligation to do this because they must pay a fee to undergo the process). There is also a Better Business Bureau rating system for all businesses even if they are not accredited (an A-F report card) and that rating is based on points accumulated within16 different categories. Plus, you can get more information on the business as far as contacts and a map of their location. Lastly, you can become educated on the latest *scams* by seeing if there are any alerts that may be affecting the gold and silver trading industry in general.

Next, go to the ICTA website. The *Industry Council for Tangible Assets* is the U.S. trade association for all businesses that trade in gold and silver as well as many other valuables. See if the business you are researching is a member. You can search by state or specialty. Even better, the ICTA will give you a list of specialists in your state that you can cross-reference with the Better Business Bureau.

> The ICTA is also a powerful lobbyist; so, if there are bills in Congress addressing the buying, selling, or ownership of precious metals, you can bet this association will be on top of it. The latest industry info is prominent on their website.

Once you have narrowed down a short list of private dealers, visit their websites so that you have an idea of what you would like to purchase, or at least have a firm idea of what kind of investment you would like to inquire about. Next, *verify the prices of gold and silver* online. You want to know what the market is doing before you buy so you can separate, and evaluate, the dealer markups from the spot price. Just as important, you must decide where you are going to store your precious metals before you take delivery (more on storage in chapter 5).

Call up and talk to the dealer; ask some questions. The dealer that you want to do business with will take the time to figure out *why* you are investing in physical gold and silver, not just try to sell you the cheapest product. You certainly will want a dealer that you like with a gut-feeling, but part of that feeling will come from the fact that this dealer will know you are knowledgeable about the basics and that you have done your homework.

Questions for Dealers

- What are the premiums, or markups, that you will be paying over the present market price of gold and silver?
- Is the price guaranteed or will the price change if gold goes up or down within the day? Remember: the price of gold can change by one hundred dollars or more in a single 24 hour period. The dealer will usually be giving

you the *spot price,* or, the immediate price if you pay within 24 hours. Check to see what the dealer's policy is regarding price changes within 24-48 hours. Then, *verify prices* by calling at least three dealers within three hours, all the time keeping an eye on the market price.

- What is their return policy? Letters of authenticity concerning the true value of a precious metal coin are not generally given to customers upon purchase (they are, however, attached with a product from a government mint). Remember, all reputable dealers have a return policy. Investigate this policy to make sure that you are guaranteed 100% satisfaction.

- How will the precious metal be delivered? If it goes by U.S. Postal Service it has to be registered and insured. Or, if a private carrier brings your investment, are they fully insured? Either way, you want to make sure that delivery is completed *"signature required."* Also, make sure to get a delivery date confirmation before you pay.

- Finally, is the cost of the shipping included in the final sale price?

If you visit the dealer in person make sure you receive a receipt and keep it safe for as long as you own your gold. If you are doing business over the phone make sure you understand when and how that receipt is coming to you.

If you are not satisfied with a dealer through your phone conversation; if the dealer tries to send you packets of information through the mail *without* ascertaining your needs; or, if the dealer keeps calling you back attempting to make a sale; you can rest assured that they don't have your best interests in mind, only theirs. Drop this dealer from future consideration. There are too many reputable gold and silver dealers to choose from that genuinely want to build a solid investment relationship with their customers.

> Consider consulting trusted friends and family to see if they
> have had any good or bad experiences with precious metals
> dealers. Maybe one of their recommendations will suit you;
> but don't forget to do your *homework* on those tips first!

Okay, one more important idea to consider: decide, for obvious reasons, who you can trust with the knowledge that you own physical precious metals. You need to keep an *inventory* (with the location of your metals and your receipts) that you modify with each additional purchase. At least one trusted person will need to know where that inventory list is.

Review: Precious Metal Dealers

- Decide why you want to invest in gold or silver and then decide what you think the best way to achieve your goals would be. Share these goals with your chosen pool of dealers.
- Do your research! With the internet as your primary tool there is no excuse for getting into a bad situation.
- Cross-check the BBB and the ICTA websites for your choices.
- Remember to call a dealer or visit and ask important questions about their spot price, markup, and delivery and return policies.

Brokerage Houses and Registered Investment Advisory Firms

A brokerage house, often called a *brokerage firm*, is a licensed company that buys and sells everything from commodities to securities. The broker is the "middle man". Precious metals brokers perform the tasks of buying and selling for their clients and they make a *commission* on each transaction. Remember, a person who profits from commissions has a natural tendency to suggest transactions to their clients.

If you do decide to invest in securities like stocks, bonds, options, and futures, you will need to open a *brokerage account*. If you can find a really good broker, and it definitely makes sense to spend time doing so, you can confidently buy everything from physical metals to derivatives and know the transaction will be executed well—not only because the brokerage firm has a reputation to uphold—but also because they are regulated by the *Securities Exchange Commission* (SEC).

Alternatively, you may find it more comfortable investing through a *Registered Investment Advisory* (RIA) firm. RIAs typically charge a flat fee, either by the hour or, more frequently, based on the assets under management (AUM) for each client. RIA firm revenues are not driven by commission fees and therefore they do not have the built-in conflict of interest you may experience with commissioned brokers. The RIA will typically have very inexpensive brokerage arrangements with large firms like Schwab or Fidelity where even a small client can benefit from the large trading volumes an RIA can bring to a brokerage.

Both brokers and advisors (the terms are sometimes used interchangeably) can help you with your *complete investment portfolio*. This is important because any investment in commodities like gold and silver should be an appropriate part of a well planned and thoughtfully diversified portfolio. RIAs are typically more effective in this critically important function because they most often create client investment portfolios using what's called an *open architecture*.

Open Architecture

Open architecture means the RIA can select *any* mutual fund or portfolio manager or broker to help in managing client assets. Most brokerage firms, on the other hand, are tied to a select few mutual fund families or portfolio managers because the broker has a special fee-sharing relationship with them. This limits the investment opportunities a broker will be willing (or even able) to show clients, vastly diminishing investment choices for individuals.

RIA business fee arrangements are typically based on an AUM fee paid by the client—meaning the client may pay 1% per year of the client assets managed by the RIA. This means the RIA will *only* benefit if the client's assets grow through the best investment strategy and will not gain anything by triggering numerous transactions or dealing only with fee sharing funds.

Credentials

Another thing to look for is broker or advisor credentials. The most sought after credentials in the investment brokerage or advisory business are the *CFP (Certified Financial Planner)* and the *CFA (Certified Financial Analyst)*. Achievement of either of these designations insures the client that their financial advisor has undergone a long and rigorous educational process. The CFA designation is the more prestigious of the two and is very difficult to attain. CFPs and CFAs bring a lot of knowledge to the table. Whether investing for the long-term or executing short-term strategies, clients need sound and consistent advice. You are far more likely to find these designations at RIA firms than at brokerage firms.

In general, the first thing to do is to make sure that you are dealing with a *licensed and registered* broker or advisor. You can research both at the website of the *Financial Industry Regulatory Authority, Inc.,* or FINRA. Through FINRA's broker check program you can look at a brokerage's contact info and vital statistics for the past ten years. You can then search, through FINRA, individual brokers and their licensure and registration status, as well as education, employment, and legal histories on FINRA's Central Registration Depository (CRD). Here you will be able to read the broker's or advisor's *Form ADV Part II*. This form provides a detailed and consumer friendly description of all aspects of the advisor's business and bios on professional investment employees. It is a "must do" step before deciding on a relationship. You can also cross-check a broker through your state's securities regulator. That information is available on the

North American Securities Administrators Association (NASAA) website.

In addition, you don't want to have to worry that a broker might go belly-up and become insolvent with your money; so check to see if the brokerage is a member of the *Securities Investor Protection Corporation* (SIPC). This organization will not protect you from poor investment choices and declining stock prices, but it will insure your investments up to $500,000 in securities and up to $250,000 in cash (the unused cash in your brokerage account) if the brokerage goes out of business. Last but not least, don't forget to visit the website of the *Better Business Bureau* and cross-check your choices!

> All of the research just mentioned may not net you the perfect broker or advisor, but at least you will be able to come up with a short list of reputable ones to begin the interview process. For a *list of questions* you might want to ask a broker, visit the U.S. Securities Exchange Commission website.

Fees

There are ancillary fees to consider with brokerages and advisors. Each time you open or close an account there might be a fee. Your investment portfolio might require separate accounts if you have different family members participating, if you have a separate IRA (individual retirement account), or if you just wish to keep one type of investment portfolio separate from another (this would be true if you are interested in derivatives like gold or silver futures and options). There is usually a fee for a transfer of funds from one account to the other. An IRA might contain a *custodian fee* to manage it just like a mutual fund. Also, with a broker, if you don't use your account often, or fail to keep a minimum balance, expect to pay extra.

Full Service versus Discount Brokers

Brokerage houses are a prime example of "you get what you pay for." As you do your research, you will find that the fees per transaction vary with the amount of attention you get from the firm. There are two basic types of brokers: the *full service* and the *discount broker*. With the full service broker you will get more attention and someone to hold your hand as you negotiate the precious metals market. This will certainly cost more in fees and commissions, which will cut into any profits you make. On the plus side, you will be able to call full service brokers and meet with them personally.

> You need to appreciate the fact that you might not score the teammate you need to be financially successful your first try. You may need to hit and miss a couple times to get a personality, and a talent level, that you're comfortable with.

Discount brokers are basically websites. With these firms you can certainly talk to someone to set up your account. You can also call someone and wait to get help with a technical problem relating to your understanding of the website; but, after that, you're on your own. Certainly, some people who feel that they know exactly what they want and have some experience in the market like it that way.

Discount brokers are reviewed on many websites so doing your research will be relatively easy and discount brokers deliver a quite democratic price for trading, allowing greater participation by the masses in the stock market. A low fee may also mean that although you will eventually get what you want, you're just another person in the electronic line and have to wait your turn. You may not get what you want immediately. As with full-service brokers, make sure the websites you've chosen to review are licensed and registered, and cross-check them for customer complaints.

The number of RIAs has increased significantly over the past ten years or so as the investment portfolios of baby boomers have grown. There is now over $17 trillion invested by individuals in the U.S., much of it in long-term portfolios. An improving quality of fiduciary management has evolved as client account size has grown. Most of us will eventually build a long-term investment portfolio and any asset allocation decision we make should be reviewed with a trusted financial advisor.

Review: Brokerages and Financial Advisors

- The brokerage/advisory relationship can help you find the types of gold and silver products that you want, from physical metal to securities.
- You must decide how much you wish to allocate to precious metals and then research brokerage houses and advisory businesses to find the relationship that will best help you achieve your goals.
- Cross-check brokerages and investment firms with the government and industry watchdogs mentioned in this chapter. Look for individuals with strong credentials such as a CFP or CFA designation.
- Interview three or more firms if you decide to go with a full service brokerage or RIA.
- Lastly, remember, brokerages make their money off of commissions and RIAs usually charge fees based on AUM, not commissions.

The United States Government

Purchasing gold from governments is usually a safe bet. With e-commerce these days it is not difficult to buy *directly* from the government mints that distribute precious metals in bullion coins or bars. Let's start with the United States of America's source of currency.

The *U.S. Mint* is the largest manufacturer of investment quality coins in the world. The 22-carat *American Eagle* is the best selling gold coin in the world. The Mint also sells a 24-carat coin, the *American Buffalo*, to compete with the 99% pure gold coins of other governments like the Canadian Maple Leaf. Purchasing gold from the U.S. Mint can be done directly. It is like shopping on any other online store. You can have an American Eagle gold coin delivered to your address, for your signed confirmation, fully insured, and for its market price, plus a shipping cost of under $20. Shipping costs apply to each item.

You can also go to a licensed precious metals dealer, a licensed brokerage house, or a participating commercial bank. The government sells products only to dealers who meet their standards. Strict rules apply to dealers who may buy gold from the U.S. Mint. First, a registered business must buy a *minimum* of a thousand ounces of gold. This business, according to the 1985 law that brought the American Eagle Gold coin into existence, must be a firm that normally sells a thousand ounces of gold per year in the first place. This is another way the gold of the Federal Reserve trickles down to the nation's citizens.

Domestic and Foreign Commercial Banks

United States commercial banks all store gold and silver for their customers. For United States citizens, IRS rules apply (this topic is covered in chapter 6) as far as reporting the gold and silver as assets for tax purposes.

Some U.S. commercial banks sell gold and silver bullion coins, but not all, so call the branch you wish to visit beforehand. The advantage of buying bullion coins from a bank is that first, you know the coins will be *authentic;* second, you won't have to worry about paying for delivery. You will be dealing privately with an account representative and the bank will give the exact exchange rate for the coin. Lastly, safety being a concern, you can rest reasonably assured of the *confidentiality* of your purchase.

Offshore Banks

An *offshore* bank is any banking institution that is outside the borders of your native country. The reason why an investor might wish to purchase gold internationally and store it in an offshore bank is twofold: one, the gold may be *less expensive* due to the rate of exchange and/or the tax code of that nation; two, *privacy* is important to the investor. Some gold investors don't want the IRS to know about the extent of their wealth. If an investor visits another country and sets up an account in a foreign bank, and has a large amount of U.S. currency wired to that bank, it would make sense to place that money directly into gold to be held at the foreign bank. One good reason for this may be because the foreign currency could be in trouble (like the euro, for instance). Another reason is that an investor may wish to keep his assets in the U.S. to a desirable level while investing internationally. Capital gains can then be directed to his foreign account without U.S. taxation and then converted to gold for more currency flexibility.

In Europe, for example, *Austrian* banks are well-known for their confidentiality. Austrian banks are not allowed to inspect your safety deposit boxes unless in the extreme circumstance that you are dead. Austrian banks also sell the popular 24-carat pure gold Austrian coins called the *Philharmonic*. In *Switzerland*, Credit Suisse bank is one of the most reputable banks and gold dealers in the world. In fact, their signature logo-stamped gold bars and ingots are quite popular, especially on e-commerce websites. You must be a bank customer to engage in buying gold from Credit Suisse, although this is not difficult to manage, even internationally.

With China's booming economy, *Hong Kong* has emerged as an offshore banking mecca for many international businesses and individuals. The island of Hong Kong has always been a unique haven for free enterprise since its birth as an English colony in the 1840s. It was turned back over to China in 1997 and was allowed to keep its free-wheeling capitalistic nature as a Special Administrative Region (SAR). The abundance of international currencies used to purchase products and services in

Hong Kong make owning gold in the city, and storing it in a top tier bank, desirable for corporate buyers making large-scale purchases from Chinese factories. This is because an account holder can easily liquidate gold into the strongest currency, or the currency most needed for purchasing what is required. Capital gains taxes are non-existent; an account holder won't be taxed no matter how much money is transferred from their home bank or their portfolio investments.

While it is much easier to visit Hong Kong to open an account for which to keep gold, silver, and cash, it can still be accomplished by following the instructions on the website of a Hong Kong bank, such as HSBC (Hong Kong & Singapore Banking Corporation).

Review: Buying from Banks
• Purchasing gold and silver bullion coins from banks is safe and confidential, but not all American banks have precious metals on hand.   • Foreign or offshore banks offer international travelers a method of buying and storing gold, a measure of tax relief and, depending on the bank, can make exchanging currencies a simple process.   • Offshore banks could potentially have to bend to government laws that may turn against an investor who is not a citizen of the country. As well, language and distance barriers may make an investor less comfortable than with a bank at home.

Commercial Websites

Strangely enough, websites are an extremely popular way to purchase gold. Of course, the first phrase one might think of would be, "buyer, beware." Yet, some extremely prestigious businesses and organizations have made the leap to the web and the culture of buying and selling precious metals is constantly changing to become more safe and efficient.

World Gold Council

First, check out organizational websites like the *World Gold Council* (WGC). The WGC is the market development organization for the gold industry and one of its visions is to be the "undisputed source of gold industry leadership." It's 'Investment' page gives the latest information on everything from physical gold to securities. The World Gold Council does not sell gold and is only interested in educating the consumer.

Gold Bars Worldwide

If you are interested in investing in gold bars both domestically and internationally, check out the site, *Gold Bars Worldwide*. They are an industry information service about the makers of gold bars and the world's leading gold refineries. They also have on their site an extensive review of international gold bullion coins and an excellent links page that will get you to international exchange sites and other gold market associations.

London Bullion Market Association

The website of the *London Bullion Market Association* is dedicated to what's happening in the London over-the-counter (OTC) bullion market. This website has much to say about the issues concerning producers, buyers, and sellers in the top bullion market in the world. You can also find others to trade with, providing that your *minimum* trade is 1,000 ounces of gold or 50,000 ounces of silver.

Financial Newspapers

Next, check out the websites of financial newspapers like the *Wall Street Journal, Forbes, Financial Times,* and the *New York Times.* Search for an article dealing with the information you desire. Chances are you will retrieve an article written by an expert that will offer you a crucial insight. Plus, this advice, usually by a specialist in the precious metals field, will be free advice. Now, after you've done your research on websites that educate the consumer about purchasing gold and silver, scan the top sales sites in the market.

Kitco Metals, Inc.

An industry leader in information that also sells gold is *Kitco*, short for Kitco Metals, Inc. Their gold and silver price index appears on dozens of other business web pages. In fact, over a million people visit the Kitco site each day to get real-time prices, commentaries, and to buy from the online store. Not only does Kitco sell precious metals, they are also a leading metal refinery and laboratory testing supply service. They seem to be the point-site for precious metals in both the American and English-speaking East Asian gold markets (Singapore and Hong Kong).

Bullion Direct

Bullion Direct is a clearinghouse for precious metals. Bullion Direct uses a computer system called the Nucleo Exchange that pairs buyers and sellers of precious metals in real time, just like a commodities exchange floor. Prices on their site are constantly changing in real time with the international exchange rates. They also help authenticate and ship precious metals among other services.

Monex.com

Monex.com is a company that has been in the precious metals business for over four decades, and has a website touting personalized customer service. It offers advice from global precious metals experts, sells many gold products, and also can help with storage. Monex is a site that is typical of the new hybrid discount and full service broker that offers a website platform, yet high quality customer care over the phone.

Ebay and Amazon

It is no surprise that *Ebay* and *Amazon*, pioneers in e-commerce, are also heavily involved in gold and silver trading. You can potentially purchase a wide variety of precious metals products, but one must read the descriptions of these items *extremely* carefully. There are pages of bars, bullion coins, and jewelry for sale and often the prices look very attractive; however, be careful to understand whether the piece is gold *clad*, meaning copper covered in gold leaf, or solid gold. Certainly a piece could be attractive; but, a buyer would have to decide for himself if the *veneer* of 24-carat gold leaf upon a base metal would be a wise investment.

> Another example of unclear product descriptions might be a product with a 1g next to it, to represent a *grain* of gold and not a full *gram*. Many of the products appear to be of the same ilk: grains of gold, or gold clad items that give the allure of owning the precious metal without the exorbitant cost or, sad to say, the value.

Certainly there could be an entire book rating precious metals websites. The smartest thing to do is to make sure that you don't buy from a website that specializes in gold and silver without first doing your *research*. Cross-reference websites with the various watchdog agencies discussed in this chapter. Read reviews online and speak with a licensed broker about possible hidden fees or problems with these sites.

Review: Buying from Websites

- There are quite a variety of places to purchase gold and silver, but start off with the industry association pages. These sites are mainly interested in preserving the integrity of the gold and silver trade so that all who participate benefit.
- Visit financial newspaper sites next and do a search of their article databases to make sure you've got the latest news on your interests and goals.
- Visit some of the top sites and compare prices, products, and services.
- Make sure to read product descriptions and delivery protocols carefully. Don't get scammed or, at best, be tricked into wasting money on an inferior product.

Chapter 5

Storing Your Physical Investments

The biggest concern for physical gold and silver investors is *where* to keep their investment. They want to preserve their wealth in a safe and secure, preferably secret, place. They want to be able to access their investment, even in (and *especially* in) troubled times, in order to redeem it for an effective hard currency. Lastly, due to confiscation and taxation concerns, they may not want their own government, let alone any other government, knowing how much gold and silver they possess.

The PAP Principle

The PAP principle is an easy way to remember the three important issues central to choosing precious metal storage. They are: *preservation, access,* and *privacy.* Over the long and short term, all three are crucial in deciding the correct way to safely keep hard assets that the majority of people consider quite valuable.

Preservation

The reason why people own gold and silver is to have an object of intrinsic value that is universally recognized. This object can then easily be liquidated into the wealth of one's own choice: currency, shelter, food and, in times of plenty, luxury. Gold and silver *preserve* wealth. Now, how can gold and silver, themselves, be preserved?

> It must be said that *contracted storage* does not preserve wealth—it slowly diminishes wealth away through fees. You have to decide if your particular storage costs give you the appropriate satisfaction and peace of mind to make your gold and silver worth the investment. Make no mistake; there is a cost to your peace of mind when you hide precious metals in a mattress, under the stairs, behind a water-boiler, or bury them in the backyard, even though this storage option is free.

Home Storage

Home storage is, of course, the first option. It gives you the greatest access to your wealth. The biggest drawback here is that is also gives others accessibility. Fireproof and corrosion-free safe boxes can literally be buried forever underground; but, are you able to keep the locations of your "midnight gardening" secret? Are there dangers of burglary or home invasion where you live? Is there a lack of privacy where unwanted attention might be aroused when you install a safe, or take delivery of precious metals, at your residence?

   If not, home storage might be right for you. Experts believe that a *floor safe* is the most secure home storage because it can be easily hidden, especially in the foundation of a basement. There are safe companies who make their living by creating secure home storage compartments and a representative will usually give you a free estimate on how best to secure your valuables. However, residences may not be yours forever. You might have to move. That means digging up the safe box, or extricating the safe from the floor or wall or choosing to leave it behind for the next resident. As well, people do pass away unexpectedly. At worst, your loved ones will have no idea how to access the vital wealth that has been methodically stowed away for such an emergency.

   Now, you must honestly evaluate the chances for *natural disaster* in your region. Does your neighborhood history make this a reasonable worry, or a far-fetched circumstance? Maybe you live in an area, like Southern California, that is prone to earthquakes. Environments with dry summers like Texas, New Mexico, or Colorado experience the dangers of wildfires. Do you live along the flood-happy Mississippi River? Perhaps you are in the path of twisters in Tornado Alley or coastal hurricanes?

If these scenarios do not increase your uneasiness, or if you feel like you can't let these ideas bother you, then you may, again, be a candidate for home storage. With this in mind, remember that *home insurance* companies are quirky when it comes to storing highly valuable items at home. Many companies will not insure gold, silver, or exorbitant jewelry held within your property lines, *especially* when lost through "an act of God." It is best to check and see what your insurance policy does, or does not, cover under both home invasion and natural disaster.

Bank Safety Deposit Box

Contracted storage fees are wealth eroding, but many experts admit that, from property titles to gold and silver, a bank *safety deposit box* is a very safe method of storing all of your precious items. Safety deposit boxes within the secure framework of modern commercial banking institutions create a reasonable cloak of confidentiality for normal use: gold and silver bullion coins, collectibles, small bullion bars, and jewelry. During business day hours you are free to walk in and inspect, add to, and withdraw from your safety deposit box at will and in secret.

Many of the larger commercial banks will also have the convenient service of purchasing your gold and silver in U.S. dollars or, in international hubs like New York City and Los Angeles, exchanging your precious metal assets for other currencies. Some banks sell gold and silver in bullion coins and (depending on how economically important the city) bullion bars, so that you may first purchase with a direct transfer from your account and then, drop off your purchase into your safety deposit box, and even register it as part of your IRA.

Are there *cons* to the safety deposit box? Well, there is the *fee* for the box; that surely must be debited against the idea of asset preservation. Then, because banks do not take an inventory of your personal items, your gold and silver will, most likely, not be insured against theft. In addition, the same natural disasters that might destroy your home, might not allow for quick recovery of your physical wealth from the neighborhood bank. Also, if the economy goes sour to the degree that the government declares a bank holiday, or if for that reason your bank fails, it will take time to get to your possessions.

> Lastly, but least likely, there could be another situation like the Great Depression where private ownership of gold is outlawed. You might have to empty your deposit box in front of a federal agent and sell your gold to the government at a loss.

Access

With regard to storage, the idea of *access* is simple: will you be able to get to your gold and silver in a time of need? As with preservation, one must ask questions concerning the ready *availability* of one's investment and then consider the most comfortable and appropriate storage options.

First, is the storage close by? It's no secret that when people begin to invest in precious metals, especially gold, there grows a need to physically hold and inspect the treasure. Some people call this "gold fever." Many folks can purchase bullion coins and bars and lock them away confidently with quarterly inspections. Others must have knowledge that their metals are safe daily. There's no way of knowing your "fever level" until you begin investing. Needless to say, it is a really great idea to have a storage site set up before you purchase your first items.

Maybe you have chosen a commercial bank safety deposit box. Can you walk or drive to that location? Next, you need to know how much gold you might be able to sell at any one time to your bank, and if you need to make arrangements in advance for liquidation. Or maybe you have chosen to go with the vaults of an offshore bank for *privacy* concerns (which we'll get to later in this chapter). Are you able to get to this location with a degree of ease, or difficulty? Will you need to travel by sea or air; and, if this is true, won't you need money, at least for fuel, to accomplish that task? If you won't be able to make the trip to your offshore storage, either because of physical or economic reasons, can you send a *proxy* to the facility to act on your behalf? Can business be done over the phone or internet and, again, will the offshore bank have the funds to liquefy your investment into the currency you need?

As far as accessibility is concerned, there's just no way to be absolutely sure of every minute circumstance that could possibly crop up. Gold and silver are, indeed, assets for wealth preservation in times of economic and political stress—but when that stress occurs it might take an extreme form that could negate the best laid plans. Some experts believe that the best course of action for ensuring access to your gold and silver is to *split the amounts up* between home and bank storage. This method allows for at least some of your investment to be helpful when it most needs to be.

Privacy

Gold is an asset that draws attention; usually unwanted attention. Beyond the beauty and worldliness of a piece of jewelry, there is really no reason for someone else to know that you own gold. *Privacy* is, then, the third variable in the storage equation.

Sure, you already know not to mention in casual conversation the fact that you hold precious metal assets, but your storage choice must also keep your gold and silver as safe as possible from thieves. Again, if you keep precious metals at home, it might make sense to consult with either a safe installation, or home protection company (or both) to discuss possible options in making your property secure from *intrusion*.

There are, in the 21st century, very sophisticated criminals. It seems that with every new technological advance in security there are those people who make circumventing it their life's work. The most obvious intrusion, and least dangerous for the criminal, is electronic *hacking*. As recent cases have proven, it is possible that any internet transaction can be viewed, or worse, by someone with the necessary expertise. If you end up buying gold on the internet, it might pay to install the latest *firewalls* and *anti-virus software* onto your computer.

Government taxation and confiscation are other concerns under the heading of privacy. While this book would *never* suggest to any United States citizen that they should illegally hide their wealth from the Internal Revenue Service (IRS), or circumvent the nation's tax code, there are methods that investors in precious metals have used to keep their assets from being federally scrutinized.

Some experts agree that one of the purposes of gold ownership is to not have all of one's money tied up in the U.S. commercial banking system. After all, gold and silver are *fail-safes* for the nation's currency in the event of another catastrophic economic depression. Whether the gold is kept at home, in a U.S. secure storage facility, or at an offshore location, these same experts believe that gold should not leave an electronic or paper trail. Hard records would mean that precious metals could be traced, found, and taxed (or confiscated), undermining the aim of wealth preservation.

- Preservation of wealth is the primary 21st century reason for precious metal ownership. All of your storage security considerations need to begin with this idea. Next, when choosing a storage option, weigh its cost value against what it offers you in peace of mind.
- When making a storage decision, determine how accessible your gold might be under reasonable scenarios.
- Decide how important privacy is to you when investing in gold and silver. Think about how this might affect your storage choice.
- Have a place to store your gold before you buy it.
- Always have an available inventory of your precious metal assets and, if possible, trust someone else with this information in case of emergency.

Contract Storage

Another good acronym to remember when storing your gold and silver in a professional secure storage facility is *SSL*: *size*, *security*, and *liquidity*. Since some precious metal bars are very heavy (gold is an extremely dense metal and exceedingly heavy for its size), a precious metal storage facility should be a seriously considered option. Security is enhanced at storage vaults specializing in precious metals and many offer insurance programs to protect your investment. Liquidity is also heightened for the reason that the most advanced storage facilities give 24 hour access to your private account. You can also buy and sell your bullion with a home computer, or cell phone application, through your purchased e-account.

There are a few costs to be factored in when transferring gold to one of these professional facilities. You may have to organize both *secure transportation* and *security personnel* if a large amount of gold is to be transferred. As well, gold bars need to be professionally *assayed* and *verified* before they are again sold to other investors, or liquidated by an institution for cash—another expense to be considered.

Make sure your facility is registered with local business authorities. Some storage facilities are registered with COMEX and/or the London Bullion Market Association (LBMA). Also, do your homework and check the Better Business Bureau website for complaints. There are many stories of storage facilities keeping only a small percentage of gold on hand and leasing your assets to mining companies trying to cover their *forward sales*. These are sales made by the mining companies before the precious metal ore is excavated in order to keep a cash flow to meet payroll and other costs. Leasing your precious metals at their storage facility will make a profit for the facility but it will also mean that your gold is not where it was said to be. If you need your gold, it may not be there. Always read your storage contract thoroughly, before signing it, to ensure against choosing a facility where this may be happening.

Types of Accounts

Remember that precious metals are *fungible*, meaning that an ounce of gold is interchangeable for another ounce of gold of the same quality. It all looks the same and, if it is of the same purity, is interchangeable within the global market. When you purchase gold or silver online and you never see the actual metal, or you transfer the metal you own to a storage facility, you need to take the concept of fungibility into account. In other words, is the precious metal product that you've purchased really only yours to hold?

There are three types of accounts at both commercial banking and private storage facilities: unallocated, allocated, and segregated-allocated.

Unallocated

Buying gold in an *unallocated* account means that you own *part or a percentage* of the gold within an institution's vault. Unallocated gold is the least expensive option for storage, with frequently zero-to-little cost. However, unallocated deposits most often get lent out in order to provide profits for the storage facility. That's because (one) precious metals of the same purity are interchangeable; and (two), you most likely will not visit the facility to inspect an unallocated account and, if you do, any gold that is displayed will legally suit you. Unallocated gold and silver also makes liquidation more difficult if the storage facility only has so much gold on hand. You usually have to give a storage facility plenty of time before you convert your unallocated gold into cash.

Allocated

Allocated gold storage means that you have bullion bars and coins that belong to you specifically. Usually there are *inventoried serial numbers* that are provided to the customer and, when the customer is compelled to inspect his assets, those exact bars are brought out. Sometimes however, allocated accounts may not have specific bars, just weights. In this case, your assets will be kept in a common vault with the belongings of other customers and when you need to inspect or liquidate, the weight of what you own will be brought to you. Because the storage facility must keep enough gold and silver on hand to cover all accounts, allocated accounts do cost more to maintain.

Segregated-Allocated

Segregated-allocated accounts are the most expensive, but most desirable for security and liquidation reasons. You might think that this type of account can be as simple as a safety deposit box; however, in segregated-allocated storage your assets are inventoried appropriately and then segregated into a *separate storage space* to await your visit. High-end storage facilities, used by the better online precious metals brokers, often suggest these expensive segregated accounts to customers. One reason is that, in order to create the allocated or segregated-allocated account, the gold and silver must be assayed for purity and the value of the metal must be verified. So, if the gold and silver are sold to another of the broker's customers, or converted to cash, the facility's bullion never moves and does not require expensive transport or another assay.

Review: Contract Storage
<ul><li>Another acronym to remember when choosing an outside storage area is SSL: the size of your deposit, the security being provided for your deposit, and the ease of liquidity for your deposit.</li><li>There are three types of accounts: unallocated, allocated, and segregated-allocated. Each offers pros and cons, but segregated-allocated is the best, and the most expensive.</li></ul>

Storage Security Technology

This book does not aim to tout the advantages of one storage facility over another. Nevertheless, you should know that 21st century storage facilities, like e-businesses, are always evolving. One new idea, or gimmick, can turn into a desirable trend and a customer magnet.

It must be remembered that storage facilities are *for-profit* businesses and the same cross-checking for integrity should apply. Make sure that the storage business is bonded and fully insured. Especially, *make sure you read the contract before signing* to examine both liability and responsibility in case of disaster, or in the event the facility should close.

A standard indoor storage business, suitable for precious metals, provides a fire-proof and climate-controlled space, with security codes for your own entrance. Some of the lower-end facilities offer a variety of vault sizes to store your assets, everything from safety deposit boxes to interior spaces able to store classic cars. Many storage businesses now advertise that they provide 24 hour guards and surveillance. The trend, nowadays, is certainly privacy or "non-governmental, anonymous" accounts. Some businesses also stress that their facilities are used by both national and international clients.

The next step up in facilities might be in *customer recognition technology*. Two of the latest hi-tech options would have been seen only in spy movies just ten years ago: the iris scan opens the door to the main facility if your eye matches the pattern on the account; and the thumb scan accepts only your fingerprint and no one else's. These identification methods are usually utilized in tandem with keys and magnetic slide cards that can easily be stolen or lost. Of course, this doesn't always allow for the contingency that you just might not be available and still, sincerely, need your gold. Unless someone you trust is on the account, you won't be able to send a proxy to complete your business needs.

RoboVault is unique enough to mention in this book because it positions itself as the cutting edge choice in upscale storage facilities. Built next to Fort Lauderdale, Florida's international airport, this business touts itself as an "ultra-secure high-tech, hurricane-resistant private storage facility." RoboVault advertises that its facility can withstand a Cat 5 hurricane (Hurricane Katrina, the 2005 storm that destroyed New Orleans, was a category 5 storm) and is pressurized to protect against sustained winds of 200 miles an hour. All of its storage spaces are at least 16 feet above ground to arm against hurricane storm surges. A generator allows RoboVault to operate for two weeks after a power outage.

The business gets its name because of the technology employed to bring a storage unit of any size off a gigantic shelf and bring it down to a personal drive-in viewing area. The facility uses both fingerprint scanning technology and keys. There are motion and heat detectors, photoelectric beams, and the closed circuit monitors and security crews that high-end storage businesses usually employ. RoboVault has a precious metals depository insured with Lloyd's of London.

Mint Storage Programs

For those purchasing bullion coins there are Mint storage programs available internationally; but, as of this time, the U.S. Mint does not store gold for its private customers. You may research two notable mint gold storage programs at the *Perth Mint* in Australia and the *Royal Canadian Mints* in Ottawa, Winnipeg, and Vancouver. The Mint storage option allows you to purchase coins online and then, instead of taking delivery, have the coins held securely in an allocated storage within the Mint itself. You may then visit your assets during Mint business hours. This might be a safe government-secured option if, of course, you don't mind that the Mint may be far away from your home, or that there might be the remote possibility of government confiscation.

Offshore Banks

Offshore banks are any institutions outside of your nation's borders. They might be in the Caribbean, the English Channel, the neutral nation of Switzerland, or in Singapore. All have excellent reputations for keeping the assets of their clientele safe and, most of all, *private* from the prying eyes of government tax officials.

They are also quite expensive and normally used for the bullion bars of the very rich.

People store their assets in offshore banks for many reasons, but mostly because some nations specialize as *tax havens*, or places with little or no taxes for corporations, small businesses, or foreign investment in general. These nations, often strong economic hubs or vacation destinations, have access to international currencies and exchange markets where trade can be done within the legal confines of a stable government. Investors, avoiding the watchful eyes of their own governments, will funnel their wealth to tax haven countries because of the privacy provided by offshore banks and storage facilities. Nevertheless, the United States Internal Revenue Service and other taxation entities, as well as international law enforcement agencies, have begun to keep closer tabs on places like offshore banking and storage establishments in order to fight crime and the money-laundering that often goes with it. *When investing offshore, always be conscious of the laws on both sides of the border!*

This book will give a quick rundown of these facilities, again not choosing one over the other. You will need to visit the plentiful websites to investigate how these businesses might suit your needs. Make sure, before you sign a contract, that you see an itemized allocated amount of your assets actually describing *specific* items (as in 100 American Golden Eagles, 50 Canadian Maple Leafs, or bars of a specific weight and serial number) so that you know exactly what the business you are hiring is responsible for.

Europe

Zurich, Switzerland is a leading gold trading city in Europe. Swiss officials have become quite zealous in keeping records of all gold in the country. Swiss companies are highly regulated and regularly audited by the Swiss financial market authority, or *FINMA*, to prevent money-laundering. This allows for your assets to be fully insured. Many people, nowadays, use a thoroughly researched Swiss company to buy and store their gold for them.

Client gold is kept in allocated accounts and the client is allowed to visit the gold, and liquidate it, with proper arrangements.

Because the gold is regularly audited, you don't have to worry about a properly licensed company lending out your investment. The costs can add up, though: there are purchasing and account set-up fees; the annual storage fees that average *3/4 of a percent* of your gold's worth; and some facilities require 2 years storage cost in advance. Selling your gold, or liquefying it into currency, nets a fee of up to 2% on the total value of the transaction. Also, remember that, in Switzerland, you are dealing in the metric system (kilograms), not ounces.

Vienna, Austria is another major European banking town that famously trades in precious metals. A storage facility, like *Das Safe*, would be considered typical, with 24/7 security and surveillance, and a thousand tons of reinforced concrete surrounding its vaults. When opening an account you will have to register your passport with the facility (thus making it accessible to Austrian authorities). However, it would take an extreme circumstance, like your death, to legally allow for your personal belongings to be inspected. There is also a relatively high level of insurance available for your assets in Austria.

The *Isle of Guernsey*, in the English Channel, is home to another European hotspot for storing precious metals. Obviously the island nature of a storage unit might enhance its security. It also helps that the Isle is a tourist destination. There are companies, like Guernsey Network Securities, Ltd., that employ their own security company, besides depending upon the police of Guernsey. This facility promises that all assets will be kept in segregated-allocated accounts.

In London, the famous *Harrods Department Store* specializes in gold bullion sales. This legendary caterer and showplace for the well-heeled elite also stores purchased gold in its own highly secure vaults in segregated-allocated accounts. The business also guarantees to buy back any purchase, at the current market price of course.

Hong Kong, Singapore, and Asia

China, India, Singapore, Korea, and other Southeast Asian countries are the reasons why people would want to put their cash, gold, and silver in Asia. The ability to invest directly in these dynamic markets has 21st century investors salivating. There is also the ability to make money and store that money with little-to-no tax on capital gains. In many cases, the rule of law and private property rights have not yet reached the level of credibility investors would normally demand. It can also be true that local citizens with government connections have a great advantage. Yet, as these countries compete for global capital to help grow their economies, having wealth in the area and solid banking contacts can be a *distinct advantage*. It may very well become an Asian century, as the 20th century belonged to the U.S. The investors who are successful in Asia will be from all over the world, however, as befits modern times.

When precious metals are being stored to consolidate your wealth, you will have to conduct extensive research and due diligence, even close hand inspection, to know where to keep your assets. Having the ability to liquidate gold into a currency of choice will be a key to timely investments as the century moves forward and certainly a consideration when choosing an Asian facility.

The Caribbean

Islands in the Caribbean, including *Bermuda, Grand Cayman,* the *Bahamas,* and the *Virgin Islands* just to name a few, offer many advantages to the offshore investor. Many of the islands offer low tax rates, sophisticated banking institutions, and sympathetic governments that legislate with foreign investment in mind. Many of the larger islands offer a high quality of life, as vacation destinations and permanent residences. They have excellent infrastructures: including highways, ports, airports, electricity grids, and e-business capabilities. A downside to the Caribbean is that being the playground of the very rich, prices are exorbitant. Bermuda, for example, is one of the most expensive places to live in the world.

Review: Domestic and International Storage

- Read the contract before signing. Make sure the facility is registered, bonded, and insured. Find out how the facility will satisfy you if your assets are lost because of disaster.
- Storage facilities are becoming more and more high tech, but also high-end. Decide what you can afford to give you both peace of mind and the ability to store your gold without too much overhead.
- Mint storage programs are a low cost way to keep your foreign-purchased bullion coins. The U.S. Mint, however, does not offer this program as of late 2011. Mints like the Perth Mint in Australia, and the Royal Canadian Mint, do offer storage at little-to-no cost for your purchases.
- European offshore banks offer low tax, secure, and private options for your gold and silver storage. However, the costs associated with these storage facilities will give an advantage only to those owning bullion bars in modest to considerable amounts.
- Asian banks sell and buy gold and silver, and store it at low cost. If you wish to invest in the booming Asian economy, particularly China or India, more research will be required and, maybe, even a visit, to begin to take advantage of low-tax to tax-free investment opportunities.
- Caribbean offshore banks offer both a tourist destination and an excellent infrastructure to combine with privacy and security. These islands are also extremely expensive and have some of the highest costs of living in the world.

Chapter 6

Regulations Concerning Precious Metals Ownership and Investment

The *Internal Revenue Service (IRS)* is responsible for collecting the necessary funds to run the federal government. They do this through taxing the assets and income of the American people and its businesses. Although there has been a legal income tax and a Commission of Internal Revenue since 1862 and the American Civil War, there was always conflict with the U.S. Constitution and its power to levy taxes upon citizens. The ratification of the 16th Amendment in 1913 changed all of that. The amendment led to both a *constitutionally sanctioned* federal income tax and a restructuring of the IRS. First of all, the IRS decided it needed to get a lot bigger. Just like today there were, by the end of the 1910s, so many forms!

Today, the IRS is one of the federal government's largest agencies. For the purpose of this book we will discuss the laws that might apply to you if you decide to own gold and silver. The laws are always *evolving*, so no book can account for the most recent changes. For this reason, you need to check on the website of the U.S. Internal Revenue Service in order to remain current, so that you don't run afoul of the law. However, this book will give you a firm foundation of what the laws are in 2011 in order to ask the correct questions of IRS employees who are there to help you.

Capital Gains

The easiest thing to remember about your precious metals investments is the idea of *capital gains*. Capital gains are profits you make *from the sale* of your physical gold and silver, or your gold and silver securities (stocks, bonds, funds, certificates, and so on). For instance, if you had purchased gold when it was $1500 an ounce and you sold it for $1800 an ounce you will be taxed on the $300 you made from each ounce. Each year's gain must be reported, along with conventional income from employment, by April 15th of the following year.

If you have gold and silver securities, chances are you have a broker account. Well, that broker should send you a *1099 form* in January of the following year so that you can see your capital gains (or losses) from the year before. Remember, you need to report income from dividends, interest earned on savings or other deposit accounts, and any profits from sales you make of your investments.

It pays to keep all of your receipts when purchasing gold and silver products. The IRS is interested in the *basis* for each item. The basis is the original cost of your investment plus any extra costs, like commissions made by the brokers who sold it to you. Your capital gain from a sale is the selling price *minus* the cost basis. So, each gain you make from a sale of one of your gold and silver items must be included in that year's income.

> Check out irs.gov and the page on reporting Capital Gains for more extensive information.

Individual Retirement Accounts (IRAs)

There are several types of retirement accounts, some set up by you personally, and others that stem from your employment benefits. Suffice to say that you can place your securities in an IRA for long-term gain. If you have a traditional IRA, where your initial contributions are from pre-tax income, you won't have to pay taxes on any capital gains until you decide to withdraw funds, usually in retirement. If you have a Roth IRA, where your initial contributions are made from after-tax income, you will not have to pay any additional tax on your gains when taking distributions.

You can place physical gold and silver into your IRA. The Internal Revenue Service allows both bullion coins and bars, but the rules are always changing on what specific types are permissible. For instance, American Gold Eagle coins are allowed, but South African Krugerrands of similar purity (.916 fine) are not allowed. This restriction comes from the time when South Africa was sanctioned because of their racist policy of social apartheid. However, since the rise of Nelson Mandela and more liberal South African governments, one would expect the Krugerrand to soon be allowed as an investment allowed for an IRA. Canadian Maple Leaf coins, gold, silver, and platinum are allowed in an IRA, but pre-1964 U.S. 90% silver coins are not. As well, many collectible U.S. gold coins are not eligible either. Precious metal bullion bars of pure and approved manufacture are also allowed in an IRA.

> With the rules always in flux, it's best to check with a licensed, professional precious metals broker and a tax accountant. Another good reason why a professional needs to be involved is because the broker and the IRA account managers need to contact each other directly in order to place the product in the account.

Selling Large Amounts of Gold and Silver

The United States has always been concerned about the amount of gold and silver that might possibly leave or enter the country. The rules for owning and selling bulk amounts of precious metals may change as the prices of these commodities continue to rise.

If you plan on selling large amounts of gold and silver, you will have to report it to the IRS anytime you sell more than thirty-two ounces of gold (32.15, to be exact) or at least one thousand ounces of silver. You will also need to report any transaction of pre-1965 U.S. silver coins of $1000 or more. Nowadays, because of the emphasized attention from law enforcement agencies placed on catching gold and silver transactions related to criminal activity, if you are actually selling this much, you are most likely dealing through a licensed broker or banking institution. You will certainly discuss with that broker the IRS requirements for reporting your transaction.

By the way, there are different weight requirements for reporting to the IRS if you are choosing to buy or sell foreign physical gold and silver. The weights are considerably less than domestic precious metal so make sure you know the rules!

Coming Chapters...

Now that we've covered the properties and uses of gold and silver; the various gold and silver products available; the types of firms and businesses from which to buy physical precious metals or precious metals products; options for storing your gold and silver; and the basics of regulation concerning gold and silver ownership, we now turn our attention to the '*story of gold*'.

In the following chapters, we will discuss:
- the relationship between gold and silver and paper currencies
- the history of the gold standard
- how gold can act as a barometer for the world economies
- the big-picture pros and cons of investing in gold and silver

Understanding these issues gives the modern-day investor a glimpse into the "Why" of investing in gold and provides a context for understanding the recent sharp rise in the value of gold and what this says about the overall health of the economy.

Chapter 7

Gold and Silver as the DNA of Currency

An important part of the *story of gold* is its complicated relationship to money. Precious metals were the first true forms of money ever used by ancient peoples. When people transitioned away from *precious metals*-based currency to *paper*-based currency, the new currency was still inextricably tied to gold and silver because the paper was a *stand-in* for the precious metals it represented. Early paper money literally represented specific quantities of gold or silver and could be exchanged for the precious metals at any time; it was like a gold or silver IOU from the government.

By the late 20th century, paper-based currency was formally severed from gold and silver and no longer represented a quantity of precious metal, yet its value still remained heavily *influenced* by the values of gold and silver. One could call gold and silver the DNA of currency because there is simply no escaping the relationship of one to the other; they influence each other in subtle, yet powerful, ways.

A first step to understanding gold and silver as an *investment* is to understand this relationship between paper money and precious metals. In this way, an investor can better understand the true meaning behind changing gold prices.

The Ancient Marketplace

In ancient marketplaces, the exchange of precious metals for other valuable items was simply seen as the exchange of two commodities, one for the other. Lumps of silver and gold could be exchanged for amounts of grain or a number of animals according to the negotiations of the trading partners. Precious metals were just another commodity and, like other commodities, had fluctuating values according to the needs and relative advantage of each trading partner. What determined whether the trade was equitable was simply when both trading partners haggled to a mutually acceptable exchange. If one party to the trade had a significant advantage over the other party, the terms of the trade reflected that, rather than there being a set price for goods. This type of *barter economy* was the standard for thousands of years until people in a western portion of Asia Minor hit on a way to *standardize* (to make the same) and then to *monetize* (to make into money) gold and silver.

The Birth and Evolution of Money

Creating Standards of Value

Gold was once mined in the rivers of Lydia in what is now modern southwest Turkey. Along the riverbanks were certain volcanic rocks that we have come to know as "touchstones." When gold was scraped upon these rocks it would make a certain color on the rock—but when gold *mixed with other metals* (such as silver, lead, or copper) was scratched onto the rock, the touchstone displayed a *different* color. In this way, people began to know exactly what they were getting from a lump of metal and the Lydians went into the business of standardizing weights and quantities of gold and silver.

Around 700 B.C.E., the Lydians began producing the *electrum*, lumps of metal that were standardized at 63% gold and 27% silver. The electrum bore imperial stamps to indicate they were backed by the Lydian kings and, with little doubt as to their true value, the first "coins" became a huge success. People began accepting these coins in exchange for their trade goods and used them for buying commodities from others. Other coins, like the Shekel, weighing 11.3 grams of gold, also swept through the Middle East regions of the Levant and Mesopotamia and became popular, standardized mediums of exchange.

Bimetallism

Gold and silver have an intertwining past in economic history. Both metals are shiny, resistant to corrosion, and easily worked; however, because they are so malleable they each must be alloyed (mixed) with other metals for everyday use as coins. This is the root of *bimetallism*, or the relationship of the two metals to each other and their value within a particular economy.

Archeologists first found evidence of bimetallism in Egypt, around 3100 B.C.E. The pharaoh Menes was giving silver the short end of the value stick even then when his imperial ratio determined "one part gold is equal to two and one half parts silver in value." This is the earliest known example of our human inclination to lump these two metals together as extremely valuable and exchangeable metal commodities.

Money is Born

This new idea of money (a medium of exchange based on trust and standardization) led to prosperous regional trading centers because it greatly facilitated trade. Trades were simplified because now only one party in the exchange was purchasing an item rather than both parties. There was no need to compare the *relative* values of pottery and textiles or of spices and animals; all items had an *exact* value on market day.

Even more liberating for the marketplace was the fact that money could be stored, held onto, and saved without losing its value. Unlike crops and animals, money did not spoil or grow old. People even began working for money rather than trading their services for perishable commodities—because those perishable commodities could easily be purchased with money earned from their labor.

This new, trusted, and standardized gold and silver currency made the marketplace more liquid, which fueled economic growth. *Liquidity* is the ability of a commodity or security to be bought and sold quickly in large volume without impacting the market price; a very liquid commodity can be easily bought and sold. Currency, the most liquid of commodities, fueled ancient economies and their trade centers. These trade centers began to emerge as city-states and, later, empires.

Money, in the form of gold and silver, was an engineer of incredible *cultural diffusion*, as goods, services, and ideas spread to distant lands through trade. Gold and silver coins brought silk and spices to Europe and it was the hunt for these precious metals that later changed forever the cultures of the Americas, Africa, and Asia.

Currency Manipulation

Yet, the story of gold and silver as a medium of exchange was only just beginning in the ancient world. Each major empire began to issue their own official coins in order to spur the economic growth and development that came with a trusted and standardized coinage. As their regional trading centers flourished, most governments were content to tap into this growing wealth by simply taxing the money changing hands or by other general trade controls. However, governments soon began to realize a better way to tap this wealth was to *devalue* their official currency by putting less and less gold and silver in it. Thus, true value and standardization began to give way to *currency manipulation*.

This *devaluation* of currency is done for many reasons. Within the borders of a state, it allows for *more* money to be circulated by the government—each coin contains less gold and silver and so more coins can be made. This increase in the money supply then allows the state to exert more control over the economy through increased purchasing power—the state literally has more money to spend. The government then puts the devalued currency into the economic system by purchasing what it needs; for example, buying weapons, building infrastructure, and paying soldiers. Since all official government currency is *fiat currency* (meaning it is a medium of exchange created by an official decree and put into place for citizens by the government), the citizens of a nation have no choice but to accept and use the official currency; even if the government is manipulating its value by shorting its contents or increasing the supply.

The Evolution of Money

Jump ahead several millennia from the birth of money and its nature changes even more. By the start of the 20th century, most governments of the world had replaced their fiat currencies *made of* gold and silver with fiat currencies made of paper but *backed* by gold and silver.

People's trust in the official paper money was established by the notion that the government had stores of gold and silver to support the currency. It was understood that if a citizen brought the government paper to be exchanged for gold and silver, it was that citizen's right to do so and the government had the precious metals to honor the exchange. In this way, even though money wasn't made of gold and silver anymore, its *identity and value was still inextricably tied to these precious metals*. The paper money was seen as a convenient, thin, and lightweight stand-in for the gold and silver that it represented. It wasn't perceived as simply paper because the paper was backed by a real asset held and protected by the government.

In today's world, paper money is *no longer* backed by gold or silver; it is only backed up by one's *faith* in the government issuing the money. So, the question is: if money is no longer made of gold and silver and no longer backed by gold and silver, what exactly is the relationship between money and these two precious metals?

The Power of Good Faith and Credit

While gold and silver are no longer used *as* currencies, they are used to purchase the currencies needed for international trade. The most powerful nations, such as the United States, Greater Europe, Great Britain, and Japan are in a position to greatly influence the price of gold and silver because their currencies are so *dominant* internationally. These countries have formidable banking systems, established economic prowess, and they almost always pay off their debts to creditors.

For well over 60 years, the U.S. dollar has been the world's *leading currency* for international trade. Other trading nations purchase U.S. dollars with gold, or with their own currencies, in order to purchase goods and services from around the world. Most commodities around the globe, including gold and silver, are priced in U.S. dollars and the single largest asset held in many nations' Central Bank Reserves are U.S. dollar-denominated Treasury notes. There have been many other examples of this in history. For example, the *shekel* in the ancient Middle East, the Spanish *real* in the 16th century, and the British *pound* in the 1800s all were leading currencies of their era. People trusted these currencies for various reasons, valued and utilized them for everyday monetary transactions, and invested in them.

However, when a nation like the United States has economic troubles and periodically devalues its currency by printing more paper, global markets start to *distrust* the currency for investment purposes and may wait for another, stronger means of exchange to emerge. This is when governments and private citizens begin *investing in gold and silver*. Since gold and silver have long histories of inherent value, people consider purchasing these metals to be "*hedges*" or safeguards against economic decline. If powerful governments begin to devalue their currencies and default on their debts and are less able to participate in the global economy, will people, yet again, begin to see gold and silver as the only currency to be trusted?

An Asset of Last Resort

Many would argue that it is as an "asset of last resort" that gold finds its true value in the first decades of the 21st century. Its meteoric rise in value reflects a common, global perception that world currencies, particularly the U.S. dollar, are *under threat*.

The *"credit crisis,"* which came to a head with the Lehman Brothers bankruptcy in September 2008, tipped the largest developed economies into a severe *recession* and has left in its wake a huge global debt overhang. The global financial system came close to complete collapse and stock markets around the world sank. Massive fiscal stimulus programs and, more recently, unprecedented monetary expansion programs by the central banks of the U.S., U.K., Europe, and Japan have all been implemented in an attempt to promote economic growth.

The various stimulus programs have helped economies and stock markets to recover but most of the world's largest developed economies are struggling to pay off huge *historical debt loads*. Monetary stimulus programs in the U.S., labeled QE1, QE2, (QE standing for Quantitative Easing), and Operation Twist, as well as the LTRO (long-term refinancing operation) in Europe, have pumped massive amounts of money into their respective banking systems. This magnitude of quantitative easing (monetary easing usually takes the form of the central bank simply lowering interest rates) has never been done before and, because it vastly *expands* the monetary base, it is potentially very inflationary.

When investors distrust the stability of a nation's currency, especially a currency as important to global commerce as the dollar, they look for *hard assets of true value* that can protect their hard-earned wealth. What are some red flags that the average investor should be aware of?

Red flags that the U.S. dollar is weakening:
• After the terrorist attacks of September 11th, 2001, the nation began a massive spending spree on two Middle Eastern wars in Afghanistan and Iraq; more than $1.3 trillion dollars has been spent on these military engagements.
• Given the ever growing budget deficits under Presidents Bush and Obama, the U.S. National Debt has recently grown to 16 trillion dollars; only twelve years after the budget was running a surplus.
• The rise of the economic behemoth China as a world supplier of cheap consumer goods has resulted in an incredible foreign trade deficit for the U.S. The U.S. trade deficit with China alone has grown to $295.5 billion in 2011. The overall U.S. trade deficit with all nations was $558 billion in 2011.
• As a result, the U.S. has had to sell an ever growing amount of Treasury bonds to finance its trade and government deficits, many to foreign governments, who now own 46% of all outstanding U.S. public debt. China has been a big customer for these bonds, using its huge export-driven U.S. dollar revenue to buy them. China currently holds in its reserves $1.2 trillion in U.S. bonds, making China the third largest creditor to the U.S. government behind the Social Security Trust Fund and the Federal Reserve Bank.

In August, 2011, the U.S. government got into a huge Congressional fight about whether to raise its debt ceiling or not (it's normally a mundane, repetitive legislative step), and markets suddenly became aware of the risk of the U.S. potentially defaulting on its loans. What could happen, not only within the U.S. but globally, if the Federal government defaulted on its loans? There would almost certainly be a *massive devaluation* of the U.S. dollar. Are we heading in this direction? Neither political party seems able to bring government spending under control, and as deficits pile up year after year, the rest of the world will be ever less willing to hold U.S. dollars. People were panicking when gold reached $870 an ounce in January of 1980. How jaded have we become? On the heels of the debt ceiling debate, and with the endless partisan bickering in Washington, gold reached well over $*1,800* an ounce in August 2011!

Many people today believe that the U.S. economy is sick and getting sicker. Are we just experiencing a dip within an abnormally weak economic cycle that will naturally right itself as the country's debt overhang is decreased through time? *Or, is the price of gold trying to warn us, in advance, of a less than desirable future outcome?*

Chapter 8

Understanding the Gold Standard

Another important part of the *story of gold* is the gold standard. The basic idea behind a gold standard is that paper money is tied to gold at a set value. Since gold and silver have been used and valued as a source of currency since ancient times, it makes perfect sense that when we transitioned to using paper money, we *initially* anchored that paper money to gold. This tangible anchor instilled an element of trust and standardization but *it also stabilized the value of money and made it more difficult for governments to manipulate.* While we are no longer on a gold standard, it is important for the modern investor to understand, at least in brief, its ragged history and the arguments for and against its revival.

On and Off the Gold Standard

An excellent panorama of how the gold standard can go from an ideal situation to catastrophe is displayed by the periods from 1880 to 1914 and the years following World War I and into the Great Depression of the 1930s.

The United States had set a gold standard of $20.67 per ounce in 1834. By 1880, many of the major countries had joined the U.S. by adopting this fixed price in what has become known as the *"classical gold standard."* In 1900, Congress removed all doubt about its commitment to a gold standard by passing the Gold Standard Act, legally compelling the United States government to "maintain a fixed exchange rate in relation to other countries on the gold standard." However, over the course of the next 70 years, countries including the U.S. went *on and off* the gold standard in order to meet their own need to manipulate the value of their currency.

> When countries needed to print more money or stop the flow of gold from their treasuries, they simply abandoned their commitment to the gold standard. Yet, when their economic position was strong and their currencies dominant in the world economy, they reinstituted the gold standard to create an economic advantage over less powerful nations.

The Gold Standard and World War I

Financed by the gold standard and powered by the new wonder-fuel petroleum, the young 20th century global economy experienced unprecedented growth and free trade. Individual capitalists became richer than any private citizens in history and a vast array of technological breakthroughs led to a slew of modern inventions. However, as the wealth of nations grew so did their jealousy and suspicion of each other. Each nation's industrial *capital* (money, men, and machinery) was increasingly diverted to creating large modern armies and steel navies. This huge military build-up eventually cumulated in World War I, a European conflict where tens of millions of combatants died in four years.

In the build-up to the war, the belligerent nations such as Germany effectively *ignored the restrictions* of the gold standard and *inflated* their currencies in order to feed their war machines and pay for factory labor. Government paper became relevant only within national borders and had little value outside of them.

By the end of the war in 1919, the gold standard was also suspended, of necessity, by most industrialized countries including Great Britain and the United States; no nation that had felt the economic sting of war could allow gold to be exported for international exchange, needing its value and stability at home instead.

The peace settlement that finally ended the war brought even greater economic hardship to the countries that lost the conflict. Germany, for example, had to pay so much money in war reparations that its post-war governments had to inflate their currency even further. In order to have enough money to pay their debts, they simply printed more and more and more of it until it wasn't even worth the paper it was printed on.

A famous post-war story relates how a woman went into a market with a wheelbarrow of German deutschmarks and left it outside only for a moment to shop. When she returned, she saw the deutschmarks piled on the ground, *the wheelbarrow stolen.* Inflation had made her paper money virtually worthless.

> In this post-war environment, the losing nations could not afford to be hindered by the obligations of a gold standard; they needed the flexibility to print more and more money without restrictions—no matter how futile. The winning nations also couldn't afford to be hindered by a gold standard; they could not afford to lose gold by honoring the exchange of their paper money for the gold that backed it up.

The Gold Standard and the Roaring Twenties

With so many soldiers coming back from the war front and unable to find jobs, re-implementing the gold standard did not make sense for the U.S. government. Without a gold standard, the government had more flexibility to *stimulate* the post-war economy and so reviving the gold standard was not pursued. Instead, the Federal Reserve *increased the money supply* in order to try to reverse the post-war recession and this seemed to work.

By the mid-1920s the United States was experiencing a post-war boom. Three factors contributed to this economic blossoming: First, because the economies and infrastructures of Europe were heavily damaged from World War I, European nations were buying *massive* amounts of goods from America's farms and factories. Second, tax rates were slashed when the Republicans under Warren G. Harding took over the government in 1922. Third, the dollar was allowed in the early years of the decade to "float" (to find its own value on the international market apart from a gold standard).

The Stock Market Crash

Because the U.S. had only been at war for less than two years and had escaped the war with its economic infrastructure intact, the U.S. dollar became stronger and stronger as the Twenties roared on. With money plentiful and spirits high, the U.S. began to see intense financial *speculation* in the stock market, the repercussions of which are now well known.

The frenzy of the 1920s stock market speculation certainly caught the attention of governments; they wanted to *bring back the gold standard* and the fiscal responsibility that came with it. In 1925, Great Britain went back to a gold standard and the United States government under Calvin Coolidge soon followed. The U.S. tied the dollar tightly to gold at pre-war prices and the Federal Reserve Bank began reducing the amount of money in circulation in order to keep the dollar's value stable. But was it too late?

Unfortunately, with European farms and factories slowly coming back into production and increasing the supply of goods, prices began to drop. Producers in the U.S. were not able to cover their expenses and because of the U.S. government's monetary policy of reducing the amount of money in circulation, there was less and less money actually available to pay bills. A deflation ensued and the whole house of cards tumbled down by October, 1929.

> Re-implementing the gold standard and reducing the money supply came too late to stabilize the overheated economies. In fact, it aggravated the declining economic activity and the world was thrown into a deep economic depression.

The Gold Standard and the Great Depression

The Great Depression of the 1930s initiated a re-evaluation of the gold standard. Did the gold standard have relevance in alleviating the suffering *within* the borders of a nation? If there was only a limited amount of gold in the world and the national currency was only worth so much in relation to the price of gold, how could more money be generated to invest in projects that would put people back to work? The exasperated answer first came from Great Britain in 1931: take the country back off the gold standard. The United States wearily followed Britain by *going off the gold standard* again in 1933.

Instead of being tied to a gold standard, nations once again allowed their currencies to float. This means nations allowed the value of their currency to be determined by foreign exchange markets rather than the price of gold; a method that certainly benefits the most powerful nations. Those nations resorting to floating currencies seemed to recover sooner from the Great Depression than those who retained the gold standard through the 1930s, but it wouldn't be long before the U.S. was on the gold standard again.

Confiscation of Gold

When Franklin Delano Roosevelt became president in 1932, he instituted a wide range of legislation to battle the devastating effects of the Great Depression (his program was called "The New Deal"). Roosevelt knew that gold was leaving the country at an alarming rate and destabilizing the dollar; so, in 1933, laws were created to compel U.S. citizens to turn their gold over to banks in exchange for dollars. U.S. citizens were forbidden to own gold bullion, except pre-1933 gold coins, or gold certificates which might later be used to redeem for gold.

By 1934, the Gold Reserve Act was signed into law giving the U.S. government the right to any gold, not used as jewelry, in the country. The Federal mints stopped producing gold coins. Only Federal Reserve Bank branches were allowed to hold gold certificates. The nation was put on a limited gold bullion standard (meaning only gold bars could be traded) at $35 an ounce. Finally, only foreign governments were allowed to redeem their certificates and central bank notes for gold. No one else in the

United States could have gold in their possession except as jewelry.

> Now that the U.S. government had restored its cache of gold, the gold standard was brought back to shore up the value of the U.S. dollar.

In 1936, the U.S., along with France and Great Britain, completed a Tripartite Agreement in order to tie all their currencies to each other and to gold at $35 an ounce. This agreement depended on the Roosevelt administration keeping the dollar "pegged" to the $35 gold price. This idea of keeping *gold's value closely tied to the U.S. dollar* extended into the next decade and into World War II.

World War II and the Last Gold Standard

The economic cataclysm of the Second World War sent gold flowing into United States coffers as other nations purchased weapons, machinery, and U.S. dollars for international trade. After the war, Europe and Asia were in complete tatters and the U.S., relatively untouched. Beefed up by its immense war-time production, the U.S. had by far the strongest economy and *certainly the largest holdings of gold.*

International trade could not function properly with so many economic hubs burned to cinders and, in 1944 an international meeting was held in Bretton Woods, New Hampshire. This meeting was important for the world because it created the International Monetary Fund (IMF) and the World Bank. Just as important, this historic meeting also initiated the *last gold standard* that the world economy has known: the Bretton Woods Agreement.

Bretton Woods was vital to the United States because it pegged the dollar again at $35 an ounce of gold. Even more significant, since the economy and government of the U.S. were so stable compared to the rest of the world, *all other countries agreed to buy the U.S. dollar to trade internationally.* Nations could also redeem their dollars for gold from the U.S. Treasury (ironically, the U.S. government still kept gold away from its own citizens). The U.S. dollar became the premier liquid currency of choice. The U.S. then attempted for over thirty years to keep the gold standard of $35 intact. America entered a powerful economic golden period that lasted over twenty years.

The End of an Era

Nonetheless, again human nature took a wrecking ball to the gold standard. A quickly changing post-war world saw many nations struggling for political and economic self-determination, creating instability for their former colonial overlords. Governments began to pull away from the paternal confines of the Bretton Woods Agreement and began to develop their own ways of doing things. Nations needing more money for their building projects or an economic jolt *inflated* their paper money supplies. Incessant conflicts between borders; the Cold War between communism and capitalism; independence movements in South America, Asia, Europe, and Africa—all added to the unstable political landscape of the 1950s and 60s.

Chaos, though, only *added* to gold's luster on the open market. With so much gold leaving U.S. vaults to feed the rest of the world's desire, it became increasingly difficult to keep gold at $35 an ounce. When gold sold for $40 on the open market in 1968, Bretton Woods became meaningless. By 1971, the political push was on to, again, *drop the gold standard* and float the dollar in international exchanges. By August, 1971 President Richard Nixon's administration stopped all gold sales and purchases by the U.S. government. Wiping his hands of the Bretton Woods Agreement, Nixon ended all conversion of foreign-held dollars into gold in order to stop the flow of gold from America's bank vaults. The gold standard was relegated to the dustbin of history.

Review: History of the Gold Standard

- When it worked, the gold standard created a steady value for the U.S. dollar. This value was instrumental in establishing the stability and credibility that allowed for the rapid development of the infrastructure and industrial might of the country.
- The gold standard worked for the United States as long as it had a healthy stockpile of gold in its Treasury vaults. Other nations could then redeem their U.S. dollars for gold and, in the early 20th century, U.S. citizens could as well.

However:

- It has been, historically, very difficult to get other countries to adhere to a gold standard. There are few international laws that can be enforced when a country decides it needs to inflate its money supply.
- In order for a gold standard to work, there has to be a nation with a substantial amount of gold tying their own currency to gold. This creates a comparable value against which other countries can interpret the value of their own and other country's currencies. When the United Kingdom was the dominant economy the English pound was used for this and, more recently, the U.S. dollar. The problem with this is that the economic power of a nation naturally fluctuates; gold supplies and currency values also rise and fall.
- Nations on the gold standard who engage in war often inflate their currencies and skew the standard, eventually destroying it.
- Gold standards need to be properly planned and should not be instituted during economic extremes like market bubbles or depressions.

The Benefits of a Gold Standard

Gold and silver have historically determined the value of fiat currencies. As we have stated previously, the currency of a nation may contain amounts of gold or silver; or, the currency might be backed up by the value and amount of gold and silver that a nation holds in its treasury. For instance, if the United States set the price of gold at $20.67 an ounce, as it did in 1834, a U.S. citizen would know that their dollar was worth 1/20.67 of an ounce of gold. In fact, if the citizen wanted to redeem their dollars for gold they could, at least in 1834, do exactly that because of the gold standard.

This ability to exchange paper currency for the gold that backs it up prevents *inflation of the currency*. Inflation of currency occurs when an increase in the amount of printed money makes the printed money worth less (*devalues* the currency). It is less valuable precisely because it is less scarce.

With *more* currency in circulation, producers raise their prices in order to get what they feel is an appropriate value for their goods and services (each dollar is worth less and there are more dollars chasing the same amount of goods) and the result is inflation, or, rising prices. But with a gold standard in place backing the paper currency, the amount of money in circulation is *restricted* by the amount of gold a nation has in its vaults, the price of gold, and the standard that sets the relationship between gold and paper money.

> *In theory*, if a nation on the gold standard wants to print more money, they need to either acquire more gold to back that money up or wait for the price of gold to go down. The gold standard acts as a *brake* on the government; they can't arbitrarily print more money and manipulate the economy through increasing the money supply.

Another advantage to a gold standard is that if several nations adhere to the same gold standard, international trade becomes *more efficient*. Merchants know exactly what they can buy due to their currency's relationship to the agreed upon gold standard. It doesn't matter if Japan has the *yen* and Korea has the *won*. The two Asian countries can trade confidently with each other because merchants will set an appropriate price for their products in relation to their currency's value with gold.

A gold standard gives some *stability and predictability* to a nation's currency in several ways. It instills trust in the paper currency because people know it is supported by a *real asset of real value*. It also prevents nations from arbitrarily printing more money whenever they feel like it, devaluing their currency, and causing inflation.

Why would a nation want to print more money and devalue their currency? Well, a nation in debt may want to print more money to pay that debt off more quickly. A nation may want to print more money to fund an expansive war effort or to stimulate the economy by funding infrastructure projects. Or, a nation may want to devalue their currency so their products are cheaper than the products of other nations. A gold standard makes this kind of currency manipulation more difficult and history has shown us that when governments wanted to be freed from the restrictions of a gold standard, they simply changed it or abandoned it altogether.

The Benefits of No Gold Standard

The modern arguments *against* a gold standard might be best illustrated by today's uncertain economic environment in which the government needs flexibility in their fight against recession. A primary reason the Federal Reserve, and other modern central banks, has for targeting money supply growth accompanied by a 1% to 2% level of inflation, is that a *small* amount of inflation is deemed as more desirable than any amount of deflation.

In a *deflationary environment*, where the dollar value of goods and services is consistently going down, consumers would see a natural benefit to delaying their purchases. The longer the delay, the lower the price may go. If consumption is delayed, production must eventually slow down or inventories would build; and those higher levels of inventories would then have to be sold at an eventually lower price. Profit margins would collapse, labor would be laid off, consumption would be further depressed and the risk of *recession* or even *depression* would rise. Thus, central banks normally prefer a little inflation. But what has happened lately?

The 2008 Credit Crisis

When the credit crisis struck in 2008, banks were suddenly saddled with deteriorating, non-performing loans on their books. With a recession in place, they had no interest in making new loans because most of the people or businesses interested in borrowing money were themselves in trouble and not credit-worthy. Those bank clients who were credit-worthy had no interest in taking on new debt in a recession. Therefore, lending ground to a halt and, since bank lending is the "oil" that lubricates a properly functioning economy, the economy ground to a halt as well.

In comes the government; first with a huge *fiscal stimulus* ($820 billion) in an attempt to promote growth, and second, the Federal Reserve tried to *stimulate* activity by adding liquidity to the system through zero interest rates and quantitative easing. The Fed's main mechanism for doing this is to add reserves to the system by making them available to banks at a lower price (lower interest rates) to try to grow the money supply. But if banks have no interest in lending, no level of interest rates or quantitative easing will promote true *monetary expansion* and greater economic activity.

To get a feel for what's happening (or in this case what's not happening), we have to know how the money supply actually grows. Simply stated, it is a two-step process (very simplified explanation). First, the Fed makes high powered money (bank reserves) available to banks and, second, banks lend the money and that money then "turns over" in the economy. Normally the *turn-over rate* (called *velocity* of money) is in the area of 8 to 9 times per year. So, in practice, a dollar injected by the Fed is initially lent to someone, it is then spent in one way or another and finds its way back to another bank who once again lends it back to another who spends, etc. But when the credit crisis struck in 2008, velocity dropped from *9 to less than 4 times a year* where it has languished.

In a scramble to get money moving in the slow economy, Fed Chairman Bernanke has flooded the banking system with reserves but he can't make banks lend, and the money supply growth has not expanded as desired. Many suggest the Fed, and other central banks trying the same thing, are "pushing on a string." In this case a gold standard would not have helped. In fact, it would have *hindered* the Fed. It would have prevented the Fed from doing what they have done; and, even though the money supply is still not growing as fast as we would like, the low interest rates and aggressive quantitative easing policies implemented by the Fed have had a *positive effect* and may be the reason the economy has maintained any growth at all. With a gold standard constraining the Fed's options, the economy may have fallen back into recession.

Gold and Bubbles

But what has been the effect of the Fed's aggressive policy on asset prices, including gold? One of the unavoidable side effects of pushing so much money into the system is that, even though banks are not lending, the money is finding its way into investments. This is one of the reasons the stock market has recovered so strongly; it is one of the reasons that oil prices have jumped; and it has been particularly important to the *price increases in both gold and silver.*

Investors know that the Fed will keep interest rates low and will keep flooding the system with money and they worry what will happen when *velocity picks up again.* Many fear a spike in inflation across many currencies as central banks are unable to withdraw the excess money they have put into the system. If that happens, commodity prices will jump even higher. Thus the word "*bubble*" has entered the financial vernacular.

We saw a bubble in tech stocks in 1999-2000, primarily because far too much money flooded into technology stocks, and partly in response to the Fed flooding the system with money as the "Y2K" fears upset markets. We also saw a bubble in home prices peaking in 2006-2007 partly based on the Fed's *overly accommodative monetary policy* coming out of the recession of 2002. And, we are now seeing bubbles in gold, silver, oil, and possibly other asset prices as some of the excess reserves in the system find their way into rising asset prices.

The Fed understands this but sees it as a *necessary risk* of supporting a critically weak economic recovery. The problem is bubbles can burst as in tech stocks, home prices, and $145 per barrel oil prices a few years ago. So, there is no easy answer. Inflation could take route and gold prices could soar further. Or, constraints on growth could win out, economic growth could fall again and bubbles may burst.

Will the Gold Standard be Revived?

The Pros of Creating a *New* Gold Standard

Generally, economies on a gold standard experience much less inflation than those with floating currencies (currencies not tied to a gold standard). When a country is on a gold standard, it has to react in *specific ways* when the price of gold changes. If the gold price is too high, the government needs to buy up and reduce the money supply. If the gold price is too low, the government can increase the money supply.

Some economists and members of Congress say that the problems from not being on a gold standard arise from a *lack of accountability*. If there is no gold standard to maintain by law, a government can print as much money as it wants depending on the situation. This can result in economic cycles being artificially lengthened, greatly increasing the risk of higher inflation and creating destabilizing volatility as an overinflated economy must eventually collapse into recession.

A new gold standard, proponents say, would *constrain* the inflationary potential of an economy growing too fast and reduce or eliminate the payoffs of the speculative financial excesses that have created such powerful players on Wall Street and created chaos in capital markets. With currencies stabilized, interest rates would be more predictable, commodities price volatility less extreme, and business planning and development around the world could proceed in a more predictable way. Theoretically, this would also allow for better government fiscal management as there would be fewer requirements for budget-busting stimulus programs to help economies recover from deep recessions.

As well, there are those who feel that currencies based on a gold standard have, throughout history, provided the world with the basis for stable economies. Precious metals like gold and silver have value unto themselves for many reasons and thus, can support a currency that carries the literal and figurative weight of the metal behind it.

The Cons of Creating a *New* Gold Standard

21st century critics of the gold standard believe its time has *already passed*. They say that with real-time technology—something past cultures did not possess—commodities like gold *fluctuate* in price too rapidly. Brokers and investors can scan gold and silver's price journeys by the second, from a beach, a mountaintop, a jungle, or atop a mine. These rapid changes in supply and demand affect commodities prices simultaneously everywhere in the marketplace.

Because growing populations, abundant natural resources, and sound policies have long been associated with economic power, analysts globally are also seeing a shift in influence from the United States, Britain, Europe, and Japan to China, India, and other fast-growing *emerging economies*. These emerging countries benefit from low-cost labor and growing, young populations creating more and more economic wealth for themselves. Can the United States speak of a gold standard as if it still controlled the conversation? China, for one, appreciates its freedom from the gold standard so it can artificially drive the value of its currency, the *Yuan*, downward in order to make its plentiful exports inexpensive for other countries to purchase.

Simply put, a gold standard would need international cooperation at an unprecedented and unlikely scale. Emerging economies wanting their exports to compete in the global marketplace have learned that those countries with the *flexibility* to manage their own exchange rates have the ability to compete internationally. Those whose currencies are pegged to a specific value could be less competitive in the short-run. The largest economies, because of their economic prowess, would have to agree on a gold standard and enforce their collective will on the rest of the world.

Even with theoretical agreement that "yes, there should be a gold standard," the world would then have to agree on a redeemable price, or set of prices, for each participating currency. What price would be fair? It has been over forty years since the last gold standard and the world has changed *dramatically* since gold was under $50 an ounce. Entire continents have become empowered and have grown in international participation since the 1970s. These modern nations would never tolerate the same colonial mentality of Western dominance in economic matters that ruled during the span of the Bretton Woods Agreement.

Critics also point out that, if a gold standard was hashed out and imposed among participating nations, investors would either lose a sizeable amount of their money already spent on gold; or, at the least, have their gold for the duration of their ownership stuck at the market price set on the day of standardization. One can only speculate what might happen in the period leading up to that day. There might be a mass scramble to unload gold, or a frenzy to buy depending on the expected gold standard price. A black market for gold might spring up—weakening the gold standard over time—and gold owners and producers might resort to illegal activities to recoup their losses from standardization. Enforcement might then turn draconian.

The Likelihood of another Gold Standard

So, the question remains: With the world's currencies experiencing such destabilizing volatility, could there be, in the future, another gold standard? It is generally agreed that a return to a gold standard like the Bretton Woods Agreement is *highly unlikely* and would be legally unenforceable under current international law. As well, the Great Depression taught us that a constriction of the money supply at the wrong time can severely aggravate a recession, increasing unemployment, and delaying recovery for an extended period. Since a return to a gold standard would no doubt mean imposed constraints on the growth of individual nation's money supplies, it is highly unlikely that modern governments would agree to a constraint on their power.

If we answer that the economic future will likely move on *without* a new gold standard, then the price of gold would follow a market-driven model that could result in gold and silver prices rising as they have in the past five years. It is possible, although never guaranteed, that without new government controls, gold and silver prices could rise further—offering favorable future rates of return for the private investor. Since all signals seem to point to a continued debasement of global currencies as central banks rapidly print more money to spur growth, it may make sense for the individual investor to consider holding at least a portion of their assets in this unique metal. *If investing in gold is of interest to you, talk with a licensed investment advisor about your options and the best course of action for you.*

Chapter 9

Gold as the Economy's Thermometer

The price of gold is like a thermometer giving us a reading on the health of the economy. When the price of gold is rising, it is often an indicator of a weakening dollar and rising inflation. It is important to understand that the dramatic and historic increases in the value of gold and silver over the last decade point *not only* to a potential investment opportunity, but also to an economic climate that is becoming increasingly fragile. Owning gold and silver is one way that investors can protect themselves and the value of their hard-earned wealth from economic volatility. A modern investor can benefit greatly from knowing how to read the signals that gold prices send about the economy in general.

The Gold Fix

Every day, trade on the open market in venues such as physical spot markets, futures markets, and other derivative products, influences the price of gold in the gold markets of London, Zurich, New York, and Hong Kong. However, it is actually the five members of the London Gold Market who set the price of gold, twice a day, based on the flow of buy and sell orders from their customers. This daily ritual, in place since 1919, is called the *London Gold Fix*.

A representative each from the banks Barclays (Great Britain), Société General (France), the Hong Kong Shanghai Bank

(China), Scotia Mocatta (Canada), and Deutsche Bank (Germany), carefully study the supply and demand for gold at 10:30am, London time, and they announce to the world the AM Fix: "Today, gold will begin selling at $1,820 an ounce." Then, after lunch, they give the PM Fix. Within seconds, the gold market in Zurich, Switzerland, swings into action, it being the largest gold bullion trading place in the world. COMEX, the Commodities Exchange in New York City, participates some time afterward, followed by Hong Kong.

The price of gold reflects the various pressures of international trading each minute of the day, and there are numerous websites devoted to tracking this precious metal's performance in real time, second by second. Yet, those *most affected* are also usually the least interested or least aware; catching the radio business news with yawns while hugging coffees during the morning commute. The average person just simply does not realize how much critical information is being transmitted through gold price changes and the impact that information may have on their own lives.

It has always been true that trends in the price of gold reflect *global expectations* of inflationary pressures, geopolitical risks, and the level of investor uncertainty. The average consumer should be aware that those price changes also signal what they can expect to pay for their morning coffees and other goods whose costs are denominated in terms of dollars. *The higher in price gold ascends, the lower in value the dollar tumbles, and the higher inflation ticks.*

Inflation, Hyperinflation, and Deflation

What is Inflation?

Often, higher gold prices indicate that the prices of other vital commodities such as oil are also on the increase; although the correlation is not perfect. An increase in the price of gold often signals future inflation which can lead to lower currency values and higher interest rates on the funds needed to finance or settle international transactions. The *domino effect* comes into play as these increased costs work themselves through the entire economic system.

For example, the higher cost for fuel results in a higher cost for harvesting and transporting grain. The higher cost for processing grain leads to higher prices for meat from the animals that are fed this grain and for the refined foods made from this grain. At the end of the supply chain, these higher operating costs are realized by the consumer at the retail supermarket in the form of higher prices. This is an example of *commodity-induced price inflation*.

A second form of inflation, more insidious than commodity-induced inflation, is the kind produced when there are *both* shortages of finished goods *and* shortages of labor. When an economy is operating at full potential with little-to-no excess capacity, consumers will bid up the prices of the limited amounts of finished goods (as opposed to commodities, which are raw materials used to make finished goods). At the same time, if there is low unemployment and labor can command higher prices (in the form of higher wages) the price of finished goods is also pushed higher. This is a form of *cost-push inflation* and, unlike pure commodity price inflation, will feed on itself—it can spiral out of control.

With commodity price inflation you could experience a year when oil prices jump 20% and that would impact inflation in that period. But unless oil prices jump again the next year, the inflation impact stops; although there are ripple effects along the supply chain for a while. Cost-push inflation, however, is *self feeding* (spiraling) year after year. Wages move higher pushing finished goods prices higher; companies make a little more money but, more importantly, it means that laborers face higher prices and will fight for higher wages to cover increasing costs of living the next year. If this spiraling form of inflation takes hold, fiscal and monetary policies will be needed to slow the overheating economy to break the spiral (remember Fed chairman Paul Volker's high interest rates in the early 1980s).

"Normal" Inflation

Inflation has always been an active part of every economy. When goods and services become more valuable, their prices go up. If an economy is constantly growing, there is normally a scramble for valuable goods and services. The *U.S. Consumer Price Index* (CPI) has been monitoring the nation's inflation rate since 1950. While overall prices can rise as much as 13% in a year as they did in 1979, since the 1990s, the CPI has had an annual average jump of only 2.5%.

Governments and their central banks actually *encourage* inflation at an annual rate of between 1-3%. Economic growth abounds when the potential for profits is high and *moderately rising prices* generate more money for producers, resulting in more profits and more investment. Banks, because they practice fractional reserve banking, and only have to keep a small percentage of hard currency in their vaults (just 10% of all deposits), also participate in creating *"normal" inflation* by helping increase the money supply through their everyday litany of electronic transactions.

Hyperinflation

There are countries that have experienced *hyperinflation*, or an increase in prices and a decrease in currency value at a rate of 50% per year or more. We have already discussed the case of post-World War I Germany, where inflation rates rose between 1922 and 1923 at over 300% a month; sometimes by 41% in a single day! Hyperinflations overwhelm "normal" inflation when a nation's government attempts to pay its bills by rapidly expanding the supply of paper money. In this way hyperinflation, or the rapid devaluation of the currency, manifests as a type of *taxation* by the government. It is self-perpetuating because citizens try to spend their money as fast as they can to avoid the next devaluation caused by even more currency being dumped on the market by the government.

How do hyperinflations end? Many economists believe that, first, the government has to stop issuing money, often by dramatically increasing the price of money (via interest rates); next, spending by the government has to be controlled. Lastly, some nations, like 1920s Germany, just create a new currency. Germany made a bond available that could be redeemed for gold; yet another example of gold coming to the rescue of a civilization when it needed economic stability.

What is Deflation?

Deflationary economic periods do not happen often. They occur when the prices of goods and services decline amidst significantly slow economic activity and there is not enough velocity of money in the system to expect prices to recover. Prices tend to fall during deflations because producers are often anxious to take what they can get for a product rather than holding out with a higher price. And fewer consumers can afford to spend as the economy slows while those who can spend wait for lower prices. Moreover, deflations are rare because governments and their central banks know that when prices start to fall, production will decrease accordingly; incentive to invest in expansion will decline, and unemployment will increase. This almost always brings on a *recession* and most governments would agree that recessions will keep them in power for even less time than inflationary periods.

Hedging Your Bets With Gold

Gold is often seen as a *hedge*, or fail-safe option, during *both* inflationary and deflationary times. This is because gold stores value better than any other commodity. Gold doesn't spoil and its value is internationally recognized. When stock prices fall, the value of gold usually remains the same; or, as in recent times, dramatically rises. When the value of paper currencies weakens, gold generally rises in value. People can then use gold to purchase the stronger currencies that will be accepted for necessities and luxuries alike. In inflationary times, gold will buy more currency because the currency is devalued. In deflationary times, gold will buy less currency but that currency will be of a higher value and will, in turn, have more purchasing power. An additional benefit of owning gold in deflationary times is that economic uncertainty may cause people to rush to buy gold, simply because they can't imagine what may happen and they know gold will hold its value in the worst of times.

Purchasing gold can *protect* investors from volatile economic times because it allows wealth to be stored in a commodity that is likely to retain its value. There is little chance that its value will dissipate overnight—as we have seen paper currencies experience time and again—since financial uncertainty will drive investors into gold as a safe haven asset, upholding its value. It is a real asset of real value that has been recognized and valued by humans since ancient times. Even with all the technological wonders and complicated financial instruments we have invented, we have never diminished or detracted from the true and inherent value of gold.

Chapter 10

Review & Summary:
The Pros and Cons of
Investing in Gold and Silver

Now that you've learned about our long history with gold; about the complicated relationship between gold and money; and about our on-again, off-again experience with the gold standard; let's look again, as a *review and summary*, at both sides of gold investing: the pros and cons. Why buy gold or silver when there are so many liquid, and seemingly cutting edge, 21st century investments to choose from?

Gold during Times of Economic Instability

Let's leave out silver for a moment and concentrate just on the value of gold. Many people have physical gold in their portfolios to hedge against tough economic times. They believe that even if other investments lose value during an economic downturn, at least their gold will always have *some* value. Would they have felt the same way ten years ago when gold was averaging only $270 an ounce? Yes, they would have. This is because gold contains *intrinsic*, or natural, value. People understand gold's intrinsic value is supported by thousands of years of experience. Fiat currencies created by governments have, historically, been devalued many times; often to a value that represents *its* intrinsic value: the value of paper—whereas gold retains its intrinsic value regardless of its day-to-day relationship to paper currency.

The 2008 Global Financial Crisis

Geopolitical Uncertainties

Gold is becoming even more valuable today as the American and European debt crises cause the U.S. dollar and the Euro to recede. Gold has always been the recognized *anchor* of international exchange, especially in times of instability. Governments exchange gold for loans and debts, and they hoard gold for future endeavors and emergencies. This creates a *scarcity* that drives up gold's price. When there are international crises such as war, popular uprisings, and financial breakdowns—all of which are happening today—gold prices tend to rise in response to the downward spiral, unrest, and instability of governments and financial institutions.

It is no secret that gold prices began their recent ascent around the tragedy of 9/11. Since the pursuit of the costly War on Terror, the wars in Afghanistan and Iraq, and the uprising in Libya, the U.S. and her allies have spent hundreds of billions of dollars on wars, much of which was borrowed. So, not only have *geopolitical uncertainties* supported precious metals prices, but the growing government debt burdens to finance these wars suggest potential future inflation as governments have historically tended to inflate their way out of debt problems.

U.S. and Global Debt Burdens

Then in 2008 the global financial crisis hit, dragging much of the developed world into recession. Since then many governments have borrowed additional money to do what they are supposed to do: help *stimulate* their economies out of recession. The problem facing most developed economies is that this economic recovery is destined to be much weaker than "normal" recoveries. Financial crisis-induced recessions throughout history have always been followed by very *anemic recovery cycles*; and growth has often remained weak for a decade or more as any new wealth created by economic growth must go to repaying or writing off the massive debt accumulated over the years leading up to the recession.

While this has been happening, the U.S. government has created more debt by *borrowing* to finance increased government stimulus spending. In a sense, the government is substituting public debt for private debt. As private debt is repaid or written off, new public debt is created. Much like a heroin addict transitioning from heroin to methadone, the U.S. has transitioned from private debt to public debt, but the *debt burden* has not really gone down! "Cold turkey," the final step of actually retiring the debt overhang, is still ahead of us. Many worry that the massive monetary stimulus the Federal Reserve has engineered in recent years, in addition to extraordinary fiscal stimulus, is setting the stage for *future inflation*—i.e., debasing the currency and repaying the debt with much less valuable dollars in the future.

In fact, the U.S. is now at a point where annual *federal government deficits* are running at more than $1 trillion per year. Outstanding government debt has grown to almost $16 trillion. Compare this to the value of the annual GDP of the U.S. (the value of all goods and services created in one year) which is a little over $15 trillion.

It has been well documented in history that when a country's external debt grows to 90% or more of its GDP, economic problems and ultimately debasement of the currency become almost inevitable!

Looking back to the mid-20th century, the U.S. dollar was a currency with enough credibility to be chosen by nations as *the default medium* for global trading. Following the devastating Second World War, the Bretton Woods Agreement of the mid-1940s established a dollar value for gold and pegged, or fixed, dozens of national currencies to the healthy U.S. dollar. Nations then looked to Washington, D.C. for help by borrowing dollars from the Federal Reserve to rebuild their destroyed economies or to relieve financial trouble. Those days seem like ancient history. Presently, with the dollar valued already between 1/1600 - 1/1800 of an ounce of gold, it may be only a matter of time before the U.S. dollar is *replaced* as the default medium in the global marketplace with a stronger currency or possibly a basket of currencies.

The U.S. is now the *largest debtor nation* on Earth. If the United States were to ever truly default on its debts, as it was in danger of doing before last minute political maneuvering in August, 2011, the world's stock markets could lose all *confidence* and come crashing down. Then, the dollar's breakdown might lead to a ripple effect of financial woe throughout the world, doing harm to economies in America, Europe, and Asia alike.

As discussed above, it is conceivable that the U.S. government's incredible money printing policy of recent years could lead to escalating U.S. inflation. There have been times when a nation has inflated its currency so much that a change in the actual currency was made (Germany in 1923, Turkey in 2005), altering the landscape of its economy. Under the worst of circumstances, such a dramatic shift could occur in the U.S., *catapulting* gold and silver higher and making the precious metals the preferred currencies of value to trade for the goods and services that matter, including food.

Money Supply Explosion?

The following chart from J.P. Morgan Asset Management highlights two things relative to the Fed's most recent extraordinary money printing efforts. First, the *explosive expansion* of the U.S. Monetary Base (including Excess Reserves held by commercial banks at the Fed) from $800 billion to $2.8 trillion in the three years beginning with the credit crisis in 2008. Second, the incredible collapse of the *Money Multiplier* coincident with the uncontrolled bankruptcy of Lehman Brothers in September of 2008. When the Money Multiplier crashes, as illustrated below, it signals an *almost complete halt to normal bank lending*.

The Money Multiplier is a proxy for how often money actually *turns over* in the real economy. It is a measure of how the so-called fractional reserve system in the U.S. creates money. Although this is a vastly simplified explanation, it is primarily through the U.S. commercial banking system that the Monetary Base expands into the full money supply via lending.

Excess Reserves, Monetary Base and Multiplier
$ trillions

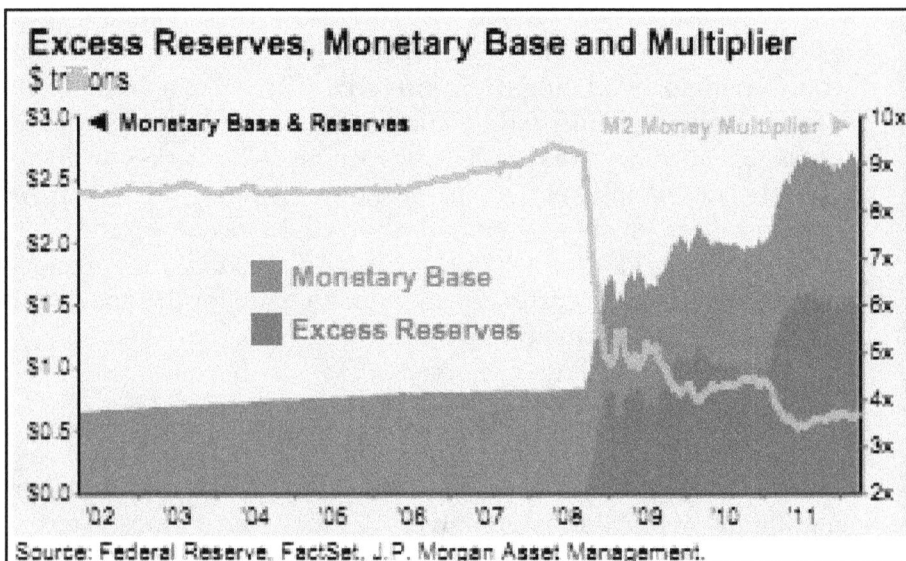

Source: Federal Reserve, FactSet, J.P. Morgan Asset Management.

Through its "Quantitative Easing" policy, the Fed has taken unprecedented steps to try to stimulate growth. The risk with this policy is that if bank lending (and the Money Multiplier) *returns* to normal levels and the Fed is unwilling or unable to reduce the Monetary Base *quickly enough*, the result could be explosive money supply growth and runaway inflation.

Furthermore, the Fed is not the only central bank engaged in quantitative easing. Take a look at the second chart (also from J.P. Morgan Asset Management) and note the *similar expansion* in Central Bank Assets engineered by the Bank of Japan and the European Central Bank. Here the expansions are measured as a percent of GDP but reflect the same extraordinary effort to promote growth.

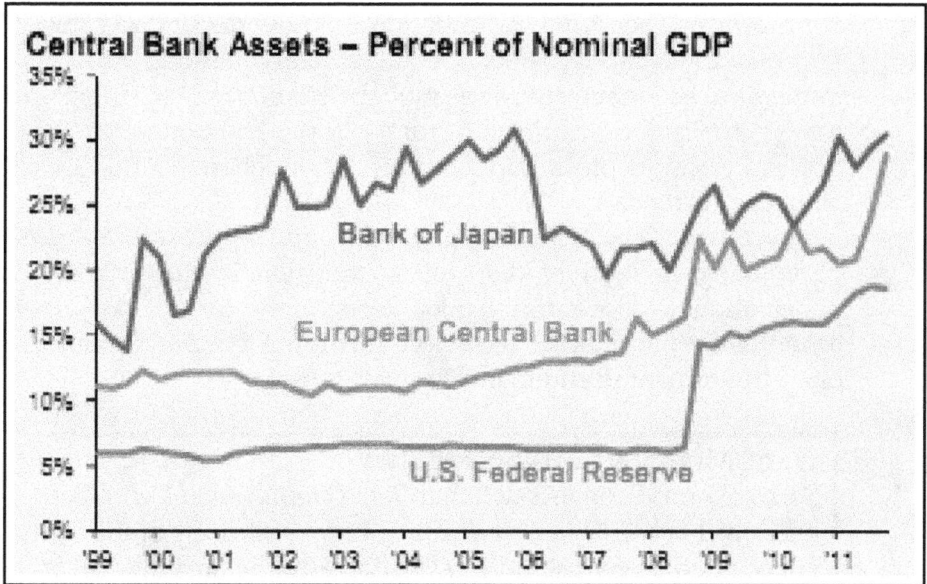

Central Bank Assets – Percent of Nominal GDP

The central banks have to rely on a two step process for their policies to work; 1. Expand the Monetary Base and, 2. Hope the excess money helps drive up the value of investments held by the public.

The objective is to create the *wealth effect*—the expected spending and risk-taking that wealthier investors will bring to struggling economies.

However, money supply expansion is not like fiscal spending in its growth-promoting impact. Stimulus in the form of *money actually spent* by the government (fiscal deficits) creates jobs and can add to real GDP growth. Fed quantitative easing makes funds *available* to banks but if *lending* does not happen, the money supply does not expand and promote job-creating economic activity and does not add to real growth.

It is clear from the data that the largest global central banks have all embraced a similar philosophy: dramatically expand the money supply in hopes that it will help spur economic growth via the wealth effect, or at least enhance *consumer and investor confidence.* The issue of inflation is now secondary. In all fairness, the central banks are all actually battling the more immediate economic risk of a global deflationary recession, and may actually be helping in that effort. The long-term risk, however, is an explosion in inflation and a debasement of almost all major currencies.

Given the continuing *economic uncertainty,* and particularly in light of the global explosion in the printing of paper money as central banks desperately try to save their economies from another recession, including *precious metals* in one's investment portfolio makes great sense!

Hard Money versus Soft Money

Some experts believe a switch to *hard money* (coins with gold and silver content) or a system of money backed by bullion (in effect, another gold standard) would hedge against the risk of an economic apocalypse and build confidence in the U.S. currency once again. These same experts say that paper currency, or *soft money,* is the currency of fiscally irresponsible governments and that there are many historical examples of this. Today's explosive Quantitative Easing Experiment could help answer whether soft money policies are always going to be with us. Yet, if the U.S. government went back to a policy of hard money, similar to the policy we had before the Yankee Greenbacks of the Civil War, many believe the economic system would be more stable and predictable, providing a better environment for all.

What would the eventual return to a hard money policy of some kind mean to an investor who had already purchased gold coins over the years, or maybe bags of real silver dollars? Of course, no one can be sure how severe the economic problems may become, but it is virtually certain that the buying power of this investor would be *preserved* and most likely *magnified.*

Gold and Silver as Tools for Diversification

An old cliché rings true: "don't put all of your eggs in one basket." Spread the money around so that if one thing fails, others can offset or balance the decline. An effectively diversified investment portfolio mixes stocks, bonds, real estate, cash or cash equivalents and alternative assets, including gold and silver. The better *diversified* a portfolio is, the more comfortably risk can be balanced with greater return expectations. This is because different asset classes do not all move in the same direction at the same time—their correlation with one another is not a perfect 1.0. When they are combined together in appropriate proportions, a portfolio of independently risky assets can actually grow faster yet be less risky than the individual assets.

Understanding Correlation

In order to achieve the highest average annual return over the *long-term*, most investment portfolios have a majority of their holdings in stocks. This has certainly been the case historically even though the last ten years have been rather dismal for stocks. Part of the reason for this relatively poor performance is because stocks were *overvalued* at the beginning of the period and some of the underperformance has been due to the great economic uncertainty we've been experiencing. Bonds and other less risky asset classes are typically *combined* with stocks to help lower the overall risk of a portfolio. Generally speaking, the higher the allocation to stocks, the faster a portfolio will grow but the greater the risk of loss in the short-term (stocks are much more volatile than other assets in the short-term).

It is also possible to diversify *within* the stock allocation of a portfolio by holding many different types of stocks: U.S., foreign, emerging market, large-cap companies, small-cap companies, and private equity funds. The problem is that when the world panics, as it did in 2002 and 2008, all stocks jump to a correlation of 1.0 with one another—meaning they behave 100% alike and all fall at once, providing absolutely no diversification benefits when a portfolio most needs it.

A correlation of 1.0 means assets move together 100% of the time. Correlation of 0.5 means the assets can be expected to move together 50% of the time. Correlation of 0.0 means you can never tell whether assets will move together or in opposite directions.

Finding an asset with a very low correlation to the stock market can be of great benefit in portfolio construction. History has shown that gold displays a *negative correlation* to stocks when it is needed most: at times of general panic and cascading stock markets; whether due to geopolitical risks, financial market risks, or increasing inflation risks. This is why gold can be such an important part of a well diversified portfolio.

No investment is completely risk free, even though it is common to refer to investments in U.S. Treasury securities as risk free. We all know that there is some small risk in Treasury securities, a risk that clearly is growing. Stocks and corporate bonds are both claims on real cash flows generated by businesses operating in an ever expanding global economy. Even with the relatively low annual stock market returns of recent years, stocks are a very good investment in the long-term. With that said, many experts agree that an investment portfolio should also include at least a *10-15% allocation to precious metals* as a hedge against dramatic economic swings, turmoil, and even disaster. The problem is you cannot always forecast these destabilizing events and it is advisable to be prepared *before* the event happens. Talk with a licensed investment advisor to determine what percent allocation is right for you.

Another point to consider is the *timing* of an investment in precious metals. The following chart shows that gold has gone up for *eleven years* in a row. This is an extraordinary run for any asset, and particularly for an asset with no associated income stream.

2001-2011 Gold Price Annual Performance Based On The London AM Fix Price	
Year	% Return
2001	1.41%
2002	23.96%
2003	21.74%
2004	4.97%
2005	17.12%
2006	23.92%
2007	31.59%
2008	3.41%
2009	27.63%
2010	27.74%
2011	11.65%

The point here is to be aware, to be patient, and to invest into any asset class over a period of time. Many call this approach *dollar-cost averaging*. You may miss an opportunity or you may end up buying at a lower average price, but it has proven an advisable process for entering long-term investments.

Diversity through Uniqueness

Another way that gold and silver can add diversity to your overall portfolio is through their unique properties. Gold, silver, and other precious metals like platinum, are considered *fungible* (rhymes with sponge-able) commodities. This heightens their ease of use in trade and their value. If a commodity has fungibility, it can be exchanged equally with other like commodities. For example, a certain grade barrel of oil can be exchanged for another barrel of equal grade. A five dollar bill can be exchanged for any other five dollar bill. An ounce of pure gold can be exchanged for another ounce of pure gold. There will be *no differences* in quality or value between the two.

In contrast, you can have two delicious, seemingly identical Fuji apples in front of you, but one might have a small bruise that lowers its value. Apples are commodities, but they are not fungible like gold and silver.

Gold and silver are also considered *hard assets* because they have a *tangible* or physical value and are able to be exchanged for other items of worth. Pure gold and silver can be brought to practically any large town or city on Earth and converted into the local currency. Even though market prices might fluctuate as they are doing today, the values of gold and silver can be as easily understood by an investor in Cleveland, Ohio as by an investor in Seoul, Korea.

Further, gold is seldom ever consumed like a barrel of oil or a pallet of lumber. Most of the gold that has ever been excavated is still in use today as a store of value (see chart below from the World Gold Council/Thomson Reuters GFMS). Even iron, with all of its utility, is not as valuable simply because of its sheer abundance. Gold's *scarcity* and ancient luster create utility even though, ironically, gold often lays un-utilized.

Above-ground stocks, end 2011 (total: 171,300 tonnes)

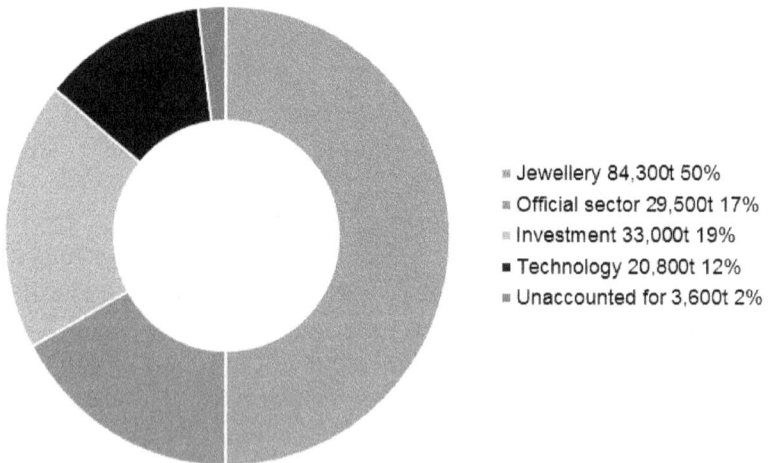

- Jewellery 84,300t 50%
- Official sector 29,500t 17%
- Investment 33,000t 19%
- Technology 20,800t 12%
- Unaccounted for 3,600t 2%

Source: Thomson Reuters GFMS
Note: Totals may not sum due to independent rounding.

These unique properties of gold can increase the overall diversity of your portfolio because gold will tend to react to economic changes in patterns that *differ* from your other holdings. As well, because of its intrinsic value and fungibility, it can be relatively easy to trade or liquidate your gold in times of need.

Gold, Silver, and Financial Market Uncertainty

A *bull market* occurs when people see bright prospects for an asset and begin to invest heavily into the object of their affection; other investors notice the trend and join in the frenzy, steadily driving up the price of the asset. Certainly, investors have been bullish on gold and silver since 2001. Both metals do well during inflationary times or during periods of great uncertainty. If an investor owns gold and the U.S. dollar declines in value or financial and economic uncertainty rises, gold becomes worth what it is today: a near record price having reached nearly two thousand dollars an ounce; possibly higher if economic and financial market chaos returns.

A Word of Caution

Financial decisions are *too often* emotional reactions. As much as we would like to think of ourselves as well-reasoned and objective, humans are animals and our decision-making, particularly in stressful times, is driven primarily by emotion. In financial markets the two dominant emotions driving decisions are *fear and greed*, and they usually compel investors to do the wrong thing at the wrong time. Thus, we must be both careful and patient when making any investment decision.

It is tempting to buy an asset (like tech stocks in 1999 or houses in 2006) when we have recently seen that they can only go up. The inverse is true about selling—who really wanted to buy stocks in March of 2009 after the crash of 2008 (yet, the S&P 500 Index is up 108% since then)? The real path to investment success is having the *discipline* to buy after extreme weakness when an asset is truly oversold and undervalued, or to sell after a long bull run when an asset is overbought and overvalued. This is not to say that gold and silver are now "overvalued," only that investors must be patient and thoughtful as to *entry and exit points*.

Thus, most professional investment advisors suggest investment holdings composed of long-term asset allocation targets, or percentage weights, for different assets in a diversified portfolio. Jumping in and out of assets based on "a gut feeling" is a sure formula for failure. Set allocation weights appropriate for *your own risk tolerance* and populate those categories with appropriate investments, and, most importantly, be patient.

In the long-term, it is possible that the world can change, and asset allocation decisions should be *revisited periodically* to respond to these changes and to bring your portfolio back in line with your investment goals and tolerance for risk. For example, in the last ten years we have experienced two stock market *crashes* followed by amazing *rallies*, leaving stocks little changed in value. As investors have run for safety, bonds have also rallied to levels that most consider overvalued and now seem at risk of dropping in value quickly at the merest hint of inflation taking off.

Central banks around the world are in the midst of the most expansionary monetary stimulus ever attempted—trying to stave off the deflationary forces of a world awash in too much private and public debt. Given these risks, a greater allocation to hard assets, particularly gold and silver, makes great sense. Decreasing the weights of stocks, and particularly bonds, in favor of precious metals at this point is what many investment fiduciaries would call a *prudent move*. Certainly, if an investor had recognized gold and silver for their value in 1999, and held on to them, these precious metals would have *out-performed*, by a long shot, any other portfolio investment.

Silver also does well during periods of inflation. This is because silver is utilized much more than gold as an *industrial metal*. When there are cost-push inflation pressures in industry, mining, and technology, silver prices tend to rise and help returns in a diversified portfolio. Silver was $40 an ounce in mid-September, 2011—near its historical peak. However, it is well to remember that, unlike gold, silver's value may *retreat* during recessions when the demand for industrial goods reaches a low point.

Gold, Silver, the U.S. Dollar,
and Foreign Currencies

It must be remembered that bimetallism is more important when the actual coinage is being made out of gold and silver—today it is not. Presently, gold and silver are commodities like sugar cane, and their prices are set in the open market, uninfluenced by an international gold standard. Unlike sugar though, gold and silver have a *direct historical relationship* to the health of fiat currencies around the world. Governments understand this fact; they also understand that, since the end of World War II, no currency has interacted more consistently with gold and silver than the U.S. dollar. This is why future U.S. government action will, in turn, affect your investments in these precious metals.

A Recap of History

From the 1944 Bretton Woods Agreement to Nixon's unhinging of the gold standard in 1971, the dollar was pegged to gold and the rest of the world's currencies were *pegged to the dollar*. Through the International Monetary Fund (IMF) and the World Bank, gold flowed from the coffers of the United States Treasury to the nations damaged by World War II, as well as to the developing nations of Asia and Africa. From the mid-1940s to the 1960s these nations became stronger economically and began to compete for international trade with newer, cheaper, more efficient products.

Germany and Japan both endured long post-war clean-ups, yet both became industrial *phoenixes* rising out of the dust of war. By the 1960s, both nations were able to claim resurgence due to high-tech industries like automobile manufacturing and electronics. Currencies like the Japanese Yen and the German Deutschemark began to strengthen into the 1980s. By helping to fund these recoveries after the war, the United States contributed to the success of its international trading competitors and, ultimately this worked *against* its own currency.

Meanwhile, for many reasons, including foreign competition, the Vietnam War, the rise of the OPEC oil cartel, and finally, the lifting of the gold standard, U.S. citizens in the 1970s suffered an avalanche of inflation and an ever-shrinking dollar. Once gold was disconnected from the dollar in 1971 there was a decade of wild *price fluctuation* (gold went from its standard price of around $40 to $800 an ounce within nine years). Gold's price dropped from a panic-driven overvaluation when Paul Volker assumed leadership of the Federal Reserve, raised interest rates, and conquered rising inflation. A long-term disinflationary period began and ushered in two decades of equilibrium. From 1981 to 2004, both the dollar and gold were relatively stable on average in their relationship to one another.

Present Challenges

Sharp price fluctuations have come back with a vengeance in the first decade of the 21st century. The causes are numerous but chief among them has been the *incredible debt* of western developed economies. Ever since Paul Volker beat inflation back in the early 1980s, interest rates have been in secular decline. As the cost of debt declined, the use of debt (leverage) became more practical for both businesses and consumers, and ultimately governments. Debt levels that were already lofty *mushroomed* in the early 2000s as consumers got caught up in the housing bubble. There were many reasons for this; not least of which was a persistently easy monetary policy.

The 2008 credit crisis and the deep recession that followed compelled the Fed to print money faster than ever before. So far, inflation has remained in check, but the risk is that prices will sky-rocket at some point and the Fed will not be able to stop them. Now, except for deflationary market forces, there is nothing to hold back the ferocious inflation of fiat currencies and ultimately an *unchecked* surge in the value of gold. What we have seen so far appears to be investors betting on this outcome and moving into gold, and lately silver, in preparation for what could be coming.

So, what does all this have to do with investing in gold and silver? Simply, *watch for U.S. government action*. Until there is government action on seriously reducing debt levels and taming spending, it is likely that the dollar will continue to be under pressure and, ultimately, that inflation will increase. Gold and silver prices will likely continue to stay at higher levels; it is possible that they could rise further still. Some experts believe that without government action, gold may reach ten thousand dollars an ounce by 2025. Does a tenfold increase sound impossible for a hunk of metal? Remember that when the gold standard was lifted in 1971, gold was priced at *around 1/50* of the price that it was in 2011.

Liquidity in Precious Metal Investments

Whether you are buying gold as a long-term investment or a short-term investment, the product will at some point need to be liquidated, or sold. The *liquidity* of an asset is the ability of that asset to be turned into cash quickly without affecting the price. Gold's liquidity has historically been very good and it can be sold anywhere in the world at one price.

If an investor needs to sell a portion of his gold, the form of that gold will affect its liquidation. There is *physical* gold one can see, touch, and pass to the next investor. There are gold stocks, futures, bonds, ETFs, and certificates that can be *redeemed* for physical gold, or cash. The various gold products available are discussed at length in chapter 3.

Gold and silver securities, such as mining company stocks and bonds, are usually held for the long term in funds or retirement accounts. Their attractiveness is based on both the value of the metals as well as receiving periodic dividends and interest payments, based on company profits.

There are two main types of physical gold: bullion bars or bullion coins. Bars most often are secured by professional brokers and then sold, or transferred, by those professionals to satisfy an investor's request. Some investors convert the bars into a fiat currency of their choice depending upon their view of the market or their travel plans. Many experts tell their clients to stay away from gold and silver bullion bars because they are obviously incredibly expensive, but also because bars just aren't as liquid as coins.

One ounce bullion coins are the most popular gold investment. Coins are small, portable, and convenient. They come in many different varieties that are sure to please both the casual investor and the gold bug, and they are relatively easy to sell. This is where silver also makes its mark. Silver coins, especially silver dollars created before 1965, are mostly silver, in wide circulation, and are always gladly accepted.

Overall, one benefit to gold ownership and investment is that physical gold and most gold investment products are *easily liquidated* when the investor needs or wants to sell their holdings.

Storage of Gold and Silver

Storage is probably the biggest *con* of owning a precious metal. However, you need to know where you're going to store physical gold and silver *before* you purchase it. Storage options are discussed at length in chapter 5.

Keeping gold at home is not always an option. Home insurance companies prefer not to cover precious metal storage in one's home. Plus, depending on the neighborhood, it could be downright dangerous to store precious metals on your property, even in a private safe. Some experts recommend that an investor should never have gold delivered to their residence at all. Stolen gold can be easily melted down so that it cannot be identified.

A bank or broker might store your precious metals for little-to-no charge and will also help to sell them when the need arises. Having a reputable and experienced broker or banking establishment taking care of one's interests is always to one's advantage when dealing with precious metals. If the objective is long term investment and it doesn't matter if the gold is not often seen, then placement in a bank's safe deposit box might be the best way to go.

However, if the objective is to have gold *at the ready* to utilize during troubled times then one has to worry if the gold is at a bank. Will the government confiscate the gold if it places a moratorium on gold ownership as the U.S. did from 1933 to 1974? Of course the investor might be paid in dollars for his investment, but the compensation might be at a government assessment of gold's value; perhaps drastically less than its current free market value.

Confiscation

The scenarios that could lead to an investor losing gold without compensation are, of course, nightmarish, extreme and, at this point, a *low probability event.* Yet, confiscation is a possibility. It has happened before, and U.S. citizens have only been able to own gold since 1975.

In 1933, President Franklin D. Roosevelt signed Executive Order 6012 making it unlawful for U.S. citizens to "hoard" gold. The administration felt that private ownership of gold was delaying the nation's economic progress and prolonging the depression. People had to be very careful with their gold possessions or risk a $10,000 fine, or ten years in prison, or both! American citizens either had to hand gold in to their banks for redemption at the price of $20.67 an ounce, attempt to smuggle it out of the country, or hide it somewhere in their homes and risk discovery and theft.

When we speak of confiscation one must wonder what could possibly lead to it in today's world. Obviously, as Americans, we think of *other nations* as the potential culprits in this scenario. Imagine, for instance, that an investor keeps gold in Hong Kong. The Chinese leadership decides it needs a large amount of gold to fund a hydroelectric power-plant in some remote part of the nation. "Why not," they say. "Confiscate the gold in *all* of China's banks!" Then, Beijing compensates the bank customers with artificially devalued Chinese *Yuan.* No one is going to stop the behemoth that is China from doing this. International condemnation will rain down, certainly; but action?

Yet, America *itself* might have to confiscate gold from its citizens if the dollar collapses in the world market and the Federal government stumbles under the massive weight of its debts. If the dollar becomes worthless paper, and the metal in a nickel is worth more than the nickel, how will an American president deal with such a crisis? Americans haven't seen anarchy on a small scale since the riots of the late 1960s, or on a large scale since the western frontier of the 1880s. When people are hungry and their currency buys little-to-nothing, they can get quite desperate.

The Great Depression is an excellent historical example, because unemployment hovered over 25%. There were widespread migrations due to dustbowl conditions in the Midwest. There were bread and soup lines everywhere and widespread despondency in the nation. The New Deal that the Roosevelt administration delivered to the troubled nation was, for that time, a *completely new way* of looking at the role of government.

The U.S. government ordered all of the nation's banks to close. The government created jobs out of thin air to put people back to work. The government created a social security network that still takes care of its citizens today, and the government *confiscated gold* from its citizens to build up its currency and repay the debts it incurred for its projects.

What if it happened today? Gold is hovering around $1,800 an ounce at present. Let's say that the U.S. government sets a very fair twenty-first century gold price of $600 an ounce for compensation. This might reign in speculation and support the dollar. However, those individuals who purchased gold in 2011 and then had it confiscated would only make back a *third* of their investment. Would they consider this better than nothing?

The point is if the economy gets dramatically or catastrophically worse, how could an American president *not* follow the lessons of the past? If you had 320 million people depending on you as the leader of the *once* mightiest nation on Earth, would you do what Roosevelt once did and confiscate gold?

Price Fluctuations

In 2001, the price of gold averaged $271 an ounce. A decade later it is averaging a little over $1550 an ounce for 2011. What can be said of *future* price fluctuations? Some experts believe gold is at the beginning of a bubble and might even reach three thousand dollars an ounce.

Is gold just an investment for *speculators*? Should it be completely avoided by those looking for "safe" investments? Gold's dramatic, historical price fluctuations have usually been the result of *interventions* by governments and their financial machines. In the past, the gold standard had been placed, as a collar on a horse, onto the precious metal in order to control it and to complete a task. Under government control, that task has always been to infuse value into the fiat currency and allow that value to translate into stable purchasing power.

Once the collar was off the horse, and gold was left to float as its own commodity in 1971, it surely felt the freedom. It rose dramatically in price, to an $870 spike in January, 1980. Yet, between 1981 and 2004, after Chairman Volker countered inflation with high interest rates, gold's price moderated and was relatively stable, averaging out at $363 over almost a quarter century. This stability continued through *two* stock market collapses in 1987 and 1998 and the previous financial uncertainty that led to these bear markets. It was only when global financial markets started to recognize the *extremely accommodative monetary policies* of the U.S.—implemented to support a shocked economy after 9/11—and the impact of tightened oil supplies on inflation, that gold started its meteoric rise to the present day.

So, again: if western central banks continue their extraordinary money printing policies and if their governments persist in running huge fiscal deficits, and the economic picture continues to look bleak or worse, it is likely that the prices of gold and silver will continue to rise.

Gold, an Investment Without Income

When an investor purchases a stock, the investor expects that the company will grow its earnings and will eventually pay a *dividend*. If earnings are strong enough, the investor realizes a return either in the form of capital gains, dividend payments, or both. If an investor buys a bond, there will be a periodic *coupon (interest) payment* producing a return on the investment. These forms of investment income are driven by successful business operations which are obviously the economic reason for the investment. When one buys physical gold, however, it simply exists—there is no income-producing activity and none is expected.

Unlike most capital market investments, gold does not provide any form of periodic payment. When you purchase physical gold you are not investing in a profit-making enterprise operating in the real economy. It's a straight *commodity* purchase. It is not consumed. It usually sits idle until it is traded again. In other words, unlike other investment products, the money tied up in gold and the potential profit to be made from gold, is realized *only when the gold is sold*. This type of non-income producing investment may not fit with every investor's goals.

So, the question remains: Are gold and silver the right products for you as an individual investor? If you believe the answer to this question is "yes", then speak with a licensed investment advisor about how to incorporate precious metals into your personal portfolio.

Review: Should I Invest in Gold and Silver?

- The world's people have long recognized the inherent value of gold and silver. These precious metals have been universally valued as a safe store of wealth, both spiritually and economically, since ancient times.
- Gold and silver are like the 'DNA' of currency. They have been used as a means of purchasing necessities and luxuries since the money-based economy began almost three thousand years ago. Gold and silver are still traded for modern fiat currencies and will, most likely, outlast government paper currencies in both utility and value.
- There are limited supplies of both gold and silver. This fact attaches a value-lifting scarcity to both of these precious metals. There is only so much gold in the world and most of it is still in use as jewelry or as a store of value. Gold's value due to its scarcity alone will likely continue to support its price.
- Another reason why precious metal prices are rising is that both gold and silver are used in many modern commercial applications apart from money and jewelry. Silver is more extensively utilized at this time; however, with new 21st century technology innovations, gold is fast becoming a crucial element in personal electronics, aerospace programs, and modern cancer treatments.
- A return to a gold standard like the Bretton Woods Agreement is highly unlikely since the level of

international cooperation needed to enforce the standard in a far larger and more complicated world would be unprecedented. Without a gold standard, a supply and demand imbalance, coupled with financial and geopolitical uncertainty, will continue to support gold and silver prices—likely producing equity-like or better rates of return for the private investor.

- Gold acts as a hedge against both inflationary times, when prices rise relentlessly, and deflationary times, when prices fall and real interest rates are high, stagnating economic growth.
- Gold and silver are the world's most trusted currencies and will most likely be accepted for necessities during the hardest economic times. It is widely recognized that, during a catastrophe, such as another depression, continuous inflation, world conflict, or even an environmental meltdown, the most valued financial commodities will be gold and silver.

Chapter 11

2011 Gold and Silver
Top Ten Lists

Top Ten Coins Worldwide for Investing

1. The American Gold Eagle (22 carat gold 1 oz. coin)
2. The American Buffalo (24 carat gold 1 oz. coin)
3. South African Krugerrand (22 carat gold 1 oz. coin)
4. Canadian Maple Leaf (24 carat 1 oz. coin)
5. Austrian Philharmonic (24 carat 1 oz. coin)
6. United States Gold Double Eagle (22 carat gold 1 oz. coin)
7. Australian Kangaroos (24 carat 1 oz. coin)
8. Chinese Gold Panda (24 carat 1 oz. coin)
9. 2012 Australian Gold Dragon (24 carat 1 oz. coin)
10. 2011 Australian Gold Rabbit (24 carat 1 oz. coin)

Sources: onlygold.com (2011); Kosares, Michael J. The ABCs of Gold Investing (2005)

Top Ten Gold Exporting Countries

1. China
2. South Africa
3. Australia
4. United States of America
5. Peru
6. Russia
7. Canada
8. Indonesia
9. Uzbekistan
10. Ghana

Source: gold.infomine.com

Top Ten Gold Mining Companies Worldwide

1. Barrick Gold Corporation (Canada)
2. Goldcorp, Inc. (Canada)
3. AngloGold Ashanti (South Africa)
4. Newmont Mining Corporation (United States)
5. Freeport-McMoRan Copper & Gold (United States)
6. Kinross Gold Corporation (Canada)
7. Harmony Gold Mining Co. Ltd. (South Africa)
8. Newcrest Mining Ltd. (Australia)
9. Gold Fields Inc. (South Africa)
10. LGL Lihir Gold Ltd. (Papua New Guinea)

Sources: energydigital.com (2011);

http://www.moneygolddiamond.com (2009)

Top Ten Uses for Gold

1. Jewelry
2. Financial Gold (coinage, bullion, currency backing)
3. Electronics
4. Computers
5. Dentistry
6. Medical Use
7. Aerospace Technology
8. Awards & Symbols of Status
9. Glass Making
10. Gold Gilding & Gold Leaf

Source: geology.com (2011)

Top Ten Silver Exporting Countries

1. Mexico
2. Peru
3. China
4. Australia
5. Chile
6. Bolivia
7. United States of America
8. Poland
9. Russia
10. Argentina

Source: The Silver Institute (2010)

Top Ten Silver Mining Companies Worldwide

1. Goldcorp Inc. (Canada)
2. Mag Silver Corp. (United States of America)
3. Coeur d'Alene Mines Corp. (United States)
4. Silver Wheaton Corp. (United States of America)
5. Compania de Minas Buenaventura (Peru)
6. Pan American Silver Corp. (Canada)
7. Silvercorp Metals Inc. (Canada)
8. Gammon Lake Resources Inc. (Canada)
9. Silver Standard Resources Inc. (Canada)
10. Minefinders Corp. Ltd. (Canada)

Source: learngoldcoins.com (2011)

Top Ten Uses for Silver

1. Coinage
2. Photography
3. Jewelry
4. Silverware & Table Settings
5. Electronics
6. Batteries
7. Bearings
8. Medical Applications
9. Mirrors & Coatings
10. Water Purification

Source: The Silver Institute (2011)

Chapter 12

Glossary

Allocated Account
An account whereby an investor has a designated amount of gold within a facility that is separated from other accounts. If bullion bars are owned, the serial numbers of these bars are listed in the account.

Alloy
A substance composed of two or more metals, or a combination of metal and non-metal.

Bimetallism
The use of two metals, usually gold and silver, at a fixed relative value, to create a monetary standard.

Bretton Woods Gold Standard
A gold standard set at the 1944 conference of 44 allied nations at Bretton Woods, New Hampshire. This standard set the price of gold at $35 an ounce and committed the United States to redeeming U.S. dollars for gold internationally.

Broker
A person who buys and sells property for someone else and receives a commission or payment for doing so.

Bullion
A weighted and stamped unit of metal.

Capital
Often described as "money, men, and machinery," capital is made up of the assets of industry invested into a project, or company, in order to make it successful or profitable. Capital is the root word of "capitalism," an economic doctrine based on the creation of profit.

Carat
Also spelled "karat;" a unit weight in precious metals and gem stones.

Chartered Bank
A financial institution that has obtained government permission to accept and safeguard monetary deposits from individuals and organizations, and to lend money out.

Central Banks
A national bank that holds gold, silver, and currency reserves; issues currency; and lends money to the national government and other commercial banking institutions; often called the "lender of last resort."

Commodities
An article of trade or commerce that is of special use or value such as oil, animals, precious metals, etc.

Confiscation
Refers to when the government authorizes laws to take private gold from its citizens either with or without compensation.

Cultural Diffusion
The spread of culture and ideas to a wide area though commerce, immigration, or war.

Deflation
Occurs when general prices fall and/or there becomes less credit and money available.

Derivatives
A financial contract that derives its value from other stocks, products, commodities, or services. The value of a derivative comes from a forecast of how well an underlying product will do on the market.

Devaluation of Currency
Results when the currency of a nation is worth less due to government manipulation. Governments will print more paper currency in order to pay its bills and to increase the money supply in the marketplace in hopes that the economy will improve.

Diversification
Investing in a variety of products in order to create a 'safety net' for the investor. If one product fails to profit, other products will maintain the stability of an investor's portfolio.

Ductile
Capable of being hammered very thinly or made into a thin wire or thread. Gold is extremely ductile.

Dumb Money
A term for an investor who purchases a product long after the value of that product has vanished or its price has risen to the point where the early investors, or "smart money," are making the most profit.

Electrum

A naturally occurring alloy of gold and silver; it was sometimes artificially created for use in ancient Mediterranean coinage.

Emergency Banking Act

A 1933 act by the United States Congress during the Great Depression that allowed only banks approved by the Federal Reserve Bank to operate in the U.S.

ETFs (Exchange Traded Funds)

A fund composed of a group of stocks, derivatives, and other investment products that all stem from the same industry or market sector. An investor might purchase a gold mining ETF, for instance, to take advantage of an upswing in the gold mining industry rather than investing in a single mining company.

Expropriation

The legal act of taking private property for government use.

Fiat Currency

A currency or monetary system created by a nation's government in order to create effective commerce within that nation's borders; i.e., the U.S dollar or the Japanese yen.

Floating Currency

A currency not valued in relation to gold but allowed to create its own value relative to other national currencies.

Fungibility

The ability of a product to be exchanged for another like product of equal value; fungibility occurs because there is no perceived difference in quality between the two products. For example, an ounce of pure gold will have all of the same properties of any other ounce of pure gold.

Futures
A contract an investor purchases that says the investor will purchase, or sell, a particular product or service at a particular price at a particular future time.

Gold Standard
A method of tying the value of a currency or currencies to gold in a fixed relationship.

Hedge
An investment term used to describe a safeguard in investing. Gold is often used as a hedge investment as its value is intrinsic and withstands market cycles.

Inflation
A steady rise in consumer prices related to an increase in the money supply that creates a loss of value in the currency.

Interest
A charge made by the lender to a borrower for the privilege of borrowing money; usually a percentage of the borrowed money. This is how the lender makes a profit.

Liquidity
The level of ease associated with buying and selling a given commodity. Currency, like the U.S. dollar, has the most liquidity. Picked fruits and vegetables have a low liquidity once they are of a certain age.

London Gold Fixing
Procedure by which the price of gold is determined twice a day by a group of five people, members of the London Gold Market Fixing, Ltd.

Mercantilism

This is the theory that a nation's prosperity comes from the value of its capital (money, men, and machinery), and its ability to export a high amount of goods while needing to import a low amount of goods.

Monetization

The creation of currency for the marketplace; making an object into money.

Mutual Funds

An investment product that contains many, diverse securities and pools the money of many investors in order to support the product. Mutual funds are managed by professional, licensed brokers who command a fee for this service.

Numismatics

The study of collecting currency, either coins or paper money.

Offshore Banks

Financial institutions that are outside one's national borders.

Options

An investment contract that gives the buyer or seller the option, but not the obligation, to buy or sell a product at the contract price before the expiration date.

Ore

A type of rock containing valuable elements including metals. Ores are refined to extract the valuable elements.

PAP Principle

A principle used for storing precious metals; PAP stands for preservation, access, and privacy, the three ideas to consider when choosing a place to store precious metals.

Pegged Currency
Currency bought and sold at a fixed rate to either an ounce of gold or a basic denomination of another foreign currency.

Physical Gold
Gold that can be handled; i.e., bullion coins or bars.

Placer Gold
Gold that has weathered away from its host rock and appears as pure gold dust, flakes, or nuggets in rivers, hillsides, and caves.

Portfolio
The combination of financial assets, including securities, cash, and physical precious metals, that an investor owns.

Securities
Negotiable financial instruments such as stocks, bonds, funds, futures, options, and certificates.

Specie
Coined money.

Speculators
People who engage in speculation are conducting business transactions with high risk. These transactions also are capable of providing significant profit depending on the level of price swings in the marketplace.

Standardize
To establish a set size, weight, and/or shape for similar objects of value. The Troy Ounce is the standard weight used for precious metals.

Sterling Silver
Silver having the standard fineness of 0.925 pure.

Stocks
A certificate of ownership in a company that signifies the buyer is entitled to a particular percentage of the company's profits.

Trade Deficit
A condition that exists when the value of a country's imports exceeds the value of that nation's exports.

Troy Ounces
A unit of measurement most commonly used to gauge the weight of precious metals.

Unallocated Bank Storage
A type of precious metal storage whereby an investor's property is not separated from the holdings of other investors. The investor using unallocated storage owns a percentage of the total amount of gold held by the facility.

Bibliography/Sources

BOOKS

Ferguson, Niall. The Ascent of Money: A Financial History of the World. New York: Penguin Press, 2008.

Galbraith, John Kenneth. Money: Whence it Came, Where it Went. Boston: Houghton Mifflin, 1975.

Green, Timothy. How to Buy Gold. New York: Walker and Company, 1975.

Holy Bible: King James Version. Grand Rapids, Michigan: Zondervan, 2002

Klebaner, Benjamin J. American Commercial Banking: A History. Boston: G.K. Hall & Co., 1990.

Kosares, Michael J. The ABCs of Gold Investing: How to Protect and Build Your Wealth with Gold. 2nd ed. Omaha, Nebraska: Addicus Books, 2005.

Kudlinski, Jim. The Tarnished Fed; Behind Closed Doors: Forty Years of Successes, Failures, Mystique, and Humor. New York: Vantage Press, 2010.
Lewis, Nathan. Gold: The Once and Future Money. Hoboken, New Jersey: Wiley Publishing, Inc., 2007.

Meltzer, Allan H. A History of the Federal Reserve, Volume 1: 1913-1951. Chicago: University of Chicago Press, 2003.

Mladjenovic, Paul. Precious Metal Investing for Dummies. Hoboken, New Jersey: Wiley Publishing, Inc., 2008.

WEBSITES

Bernanke, Ben. The Federal Reserve Board. Remarks by Governor Ben S. Bernanke: Money, Gold and the Great Depression. Mar. 2, 2004. Sept. 10, 2011.
http://www.federalreserve.gov/boarddocs/speeches/2004/200403022/default.htm

Better Business Bureau. Start Your Search With Trust. 2011. Sept. 22, 2011.
http://maine.bbb.org/

Bordo, Michael D. The Concise Encyclopedia of Economics. Gold Standard. 2008. Sept. 4, 2011.
http://www.econlib.org/library/Enc/GoldStandard.html

California's Natural Resources (produced by California Resources Evaluation System (CERES). The California Gold Rush. 2007. Sept. 3, 2011.
http://ceres.ca.gov/ceres/calweb/geology/goldrush.html

Cowen, Richard. University of California/Davis. Gold and Silver: Spain in the New World. April, 1999. Sept. 15, 2011.
http://mygeologypage.ucdavis.edu/cowen/~GEL115/115ch8.html

France24.com: International News. India and China to Lead Gold Demand: WGC. Aug. 18, 2011. Sept. 14, 2011.
http://www.france24.com/en/20110818-india-china-lead-gold-demand-wgc

Geology.com. The Many Uses of Gold. 2005-2011. Sept. 8, 2011.
http://geology.com/minerals/gold/uses-of-gold.shtml

Gold Bars Worldwide. 2011. Sept. 23, 2011.
http://www.goldbarsworldwide.com/

Gold Bullion Ingot.com. Gold Storage Facilities: How to Safely Store Your Gold. June, 2011. Sept. 24, 2011.
http://goldbullioningot.com/blog/gold-storage-facilites/gold-vault-storage-facilities-how-to-safely-store-your-gold/

The Gold Institute. June, 2011.
http://www.goldinstitute.org/

Gold Price. Daily Gold Price Index. 2011. Sept. 15, 2011.
http://goldprice.org/

Gold Price. Review of *My Swiss Gold*. June 18, 2009. Sept. 27, 2011.
http://goldprice.org/european-gold-dealers/2009/06/my-swiss-gold.html

Guernsey Network Securities, Ltd. The Facilities. 2009. Sept. 27, 2011.
http://www.networksecurities.gg/safe-custody-vaults.htm

Hamilton, James. Econbrowser. The Gold Standard and the Great Depression. Dec. 12, 2005. Sept. 14, 2011.
http://www.econbrowser.com/archives/2005/12/the_gold_standa.html

Industry Council for Tangible Assets. ICTA Index Page. 2011. Sept. 22, 2011.
http://www.ictaonline.org/index.html

Internal Revenue Service. <u>Reporting Capital Gains</u>. Updated May 25, 2011. Sept. 29, 2011.
http://www.irs.gov/newsroom/article/0,id=170634,00.html

Investopedia. <u>Pros and Cons of Offshore Investing</u>. Jul 2, 2011. Sept. 22, 2011.
http://www.investopedia.com/articles/02/020602.asp#axzz1Yj9grgMd

Kelleher, Ellen. FT.com (Financial Times). <u>The True Value of Gold</u>. Aug. 28, 2010. Sept. 13, 2011.
http://www.ft.com/intl/cms/s/2/e9378c6c-b0b8-11df-8c04-00144feabdc0.html#axzz1Y1YfPONS

Kitco.com. <u>Home page</u>. 2011. Sept. 3, 2011.
http://www.kitco.com/

Larmer, Brook. National Geographic. <u>The Real Price of Gold</u>. Jan. 2009. Sept. 8, 2011.
http://ngm.nationalgeographic.com/2009/01/gold/larmer-text

London Bullion Market Association. 2011. Sept. 23, 2011.
http://www.lbma.org.uk/pages/index.cfm?page_id=1

MacFarlane, Peter. Ezine Articles. <u>How and Why to Open a Bank Account in Hong Kong</u>. July 9, 2011. Sept. 23, 2011.
http://EzineArticles.com/6412149

Measuring Worth. <u>Seven Ways to Compute the Relative Value of a U.S. Dollar Amount - 1774 to Present</u>. 2011. Sept. 19, 2011.
http://www.measuringworth.com/uscompare/

National Mining Association (NMA). <u>The History of Gold</u>. 2011. Sept 3, 2011. http://www.nma.org/pdf/gold/gold_history.pdf

National Mining Association (NMA). <u>Historical Gold Prices, 1833 - Present</u>. 2010. Sept 2, 2011. His_gold_prices.pdf

Oldham, Jefferey David. Stanford University. <u>Why, When, and How do Mutual Funds Pay Distributions?</u> Dec. 13, 1997. Sept. 21, 2011. http://theory.stanford.edu/~oldham/publications/financial/distributions/node2.html

Only Gold. <u>A Brief History of Gold</u>.1998 - 2011. Sept. 2, 2011. http://www.onlygold.com/tutorialpages/historyfs.htm

Perth Mint Certificate Program. <u>Home Page</u>. 2009. Sept. 21, 2011. http://www.pmcg.com.au/index.php RoboVault. 2011. Sept 23, 2011. http://www.robovault.com/index.php

Rubin, Norman A. Anistoriton: Art History. <u>The Oldest Gold in the World in a Varna Cemetery</u>. Volume 7, September 2003, Section O033. Sept. 2, 2011. http://www.anistor.gr/englis/enback/o033.htm

Salemi, Michael K. Library of Economics and Liberty. <u>Hyperinflation</u>. 2nd ed. 2008. Sept. 9, 2011. http://www.econlib.org/library/Enc/Hyperinflation.html

Securities Exchange Commission. Protect Your Money: Check Out Brokers and Investment Advisors. 2011. Sept. 22, 2011.
http://www.sec.gov/investor/brokers.htm
Securities Exchange Commission. Invest Wisely: Advice From Your Securities Industry Regulators. Aug. 8, 2007. Sept. 22, 2011.
http://www.sec.gov/investor/pubs/inws.htm

Silver Institute. Silver Facts: The History of Silver. 2011. Sept.3, 2011.
http://www.silverinstitute.org/silver_history.php

Twin City Gold Coins & Jewelry. U.S. Mint Products; American Eagles. Sept., 2011. Sept. 20, 2011.
http://www.twin-city-gold.com/COINS/US%20MINT%20PRODUCTS/AMERICAN%20GOLD%20EAGLES

U.S. Census Bureau. Goods and Services Deficit Decreases in July 2011. Sept. 8, 2011. Sept. 14, 2011.
http://www.census.gov/indicator/www/ustrade.html

U.S. Dept. of the Treasury. Chronology of Events. 2011. Sept. 18, 2011.
http://www.treasury.gov/about/history/Pages/edu_history_events_index.aspx

U.S. Dept. of the Treasury. Major Foreign Holders of Treasury Securities. Aug. 15, 2011. Sept. 14, 2011.
http://usgovinfo.about.com/gi/o.htm?zi=1/XJ&zTi=1&sdn=usgovinfo&cdn=newsissues&tm=115&f=10&su=p284.12.336.ip_&tt=29&bt=0&bts=0&zu=http%3A//www.treasury.gov/resource-center/data-chart-center/tic/Documents/mfh.txt

U.S. Mint. <u>Procedures to Qualify for Purchase of Bulk Bullion Coins</u>. Public Law 99-185, enacted Dec. 17, 1985. Sept. 23, 2011.
http://www.usmint.gov/consumer/GoldAPRequirements. pdf

U.S. National Debt Clock. Maintained by Ed Hall using info from The U.S. Department of the Treasury and the U.S. Bureau of the Census. 2011. Sept. 12, 2011.
http://www.brillig.com/debt_clock/

White, Lawrence H. Library of Economics and Liberty. <u>Inflation</u>. 2nd ed. 2008. Sept. 9, 2011.
http://www.econlib.org/library/Enc/Inflation.html

World Gold Council. <u>Story of Gold: Heritage</u>. 2011. Sept. 2, 2011.
http://www.gold.org/about_gold/story_of_gold/heritage/ >
<http://www.gold.org/about_gold/story_of_gold/number s_and_facts/

INTERVIEW

Michael White. U.S. Mint Office of Media Relations & Press Inquiries. Sept. 27, 2011.
(202) 354-7222

www.ingramcontent.com/pod-product-compliance
Lightning Source LLC
Chambersburg PA
CBHW060607200326
41521CB00007B/684